Ron Ranson

WATERCOLOR
PAINTING
from Photographs

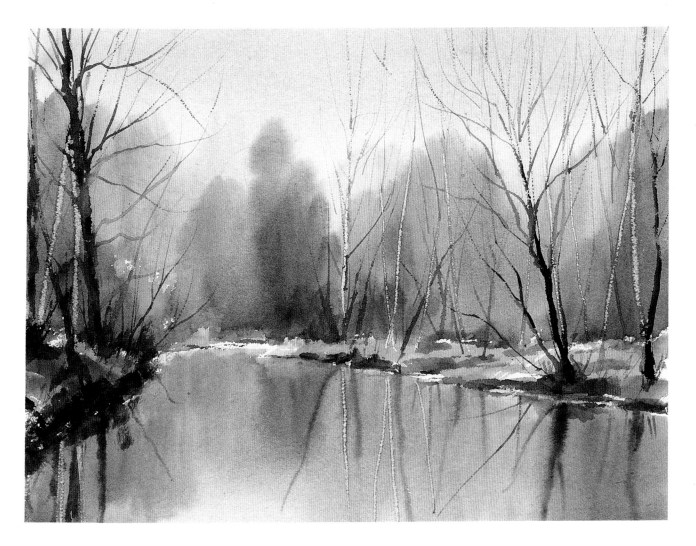

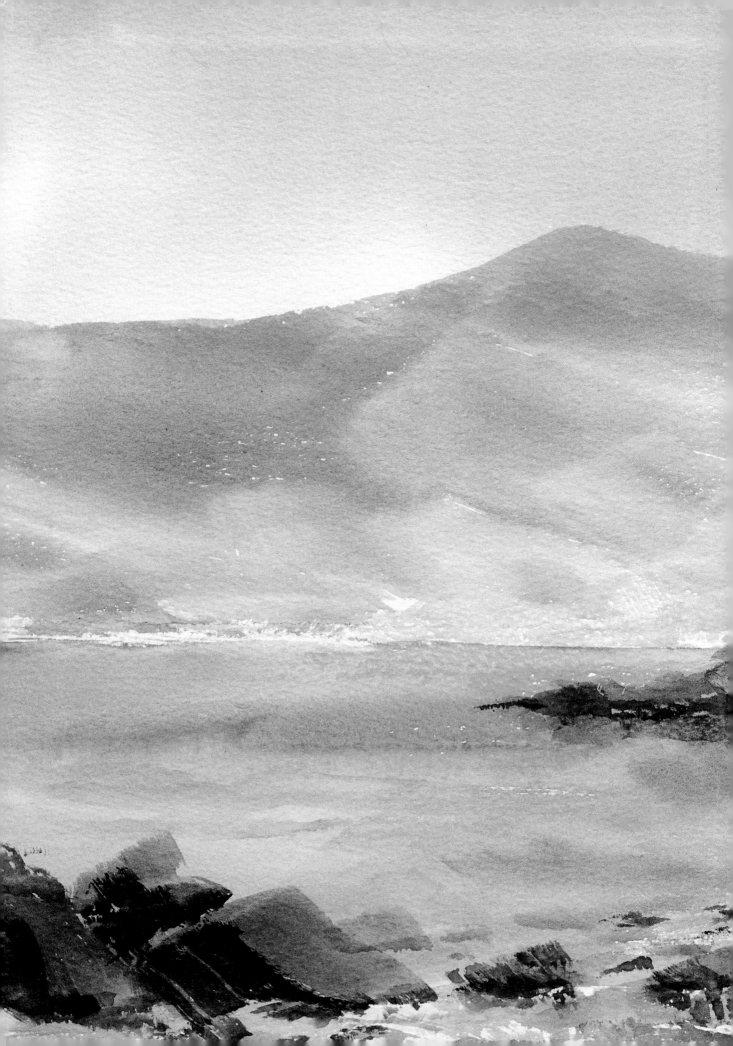

Ron Ranson

WATERCOLOR PAINTING
from Photographs

WATSON-GUPTILL PUBLICATIONS·NEW YORK

CONTENTS

First published in the United States in 1998
by Watson-Gupthill Publications, a division of
BPI Communications, Inc., 1515 Broadway,
New York, N.Y. 10036

First pubiished in 1998
by HarperCollins*Publishers*, London

1 2 3 4 5 6 7 8 9/06 05 04 03 02 01 00 99 98

Library of Congress Catalog Card Number: 97-81414

Project editor: Caroline Churton
Editor: Diana Vowles
Designer: Clare Baggaley
Photographer: Laura Wickenden

ISBN 0-8230-5709-7

Set in Plantin and Franklin Gothic
Color origination by Colourscan, Singapore
Printed in China by Imago

PAGE 1 *Afternoon Sunshine*, 12 x 16" (30 x 40.5 cm)

PAGES 2 and 3 *Greek Beach*, 12 x 16" in (30 x 40.5 cm)

DEDICATION

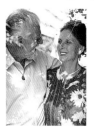

This book is dedicated to my friend Dr. Don
Fisher, a man of great humor. Not content
with finding my lost hake brush in the middle
of the Oregon wilderness, he
went on to find for me a
wife, my lovely Darlis.

ACKNOWLEDGMENTS

First, I must acknowledge
the immense help and
patience of my assistant Ann
Mills in the production of this book. My dear
wife, Darlis, has typed every word of copy
and caption, and many of the photographs
have been lent by Dr. Don Fisher of Oregon.
For all these things, I am extremely grateful.

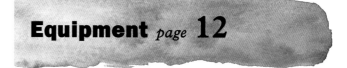
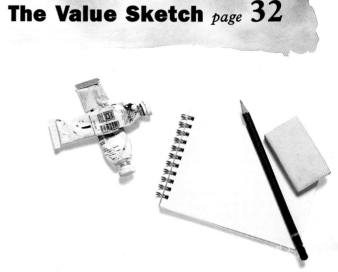

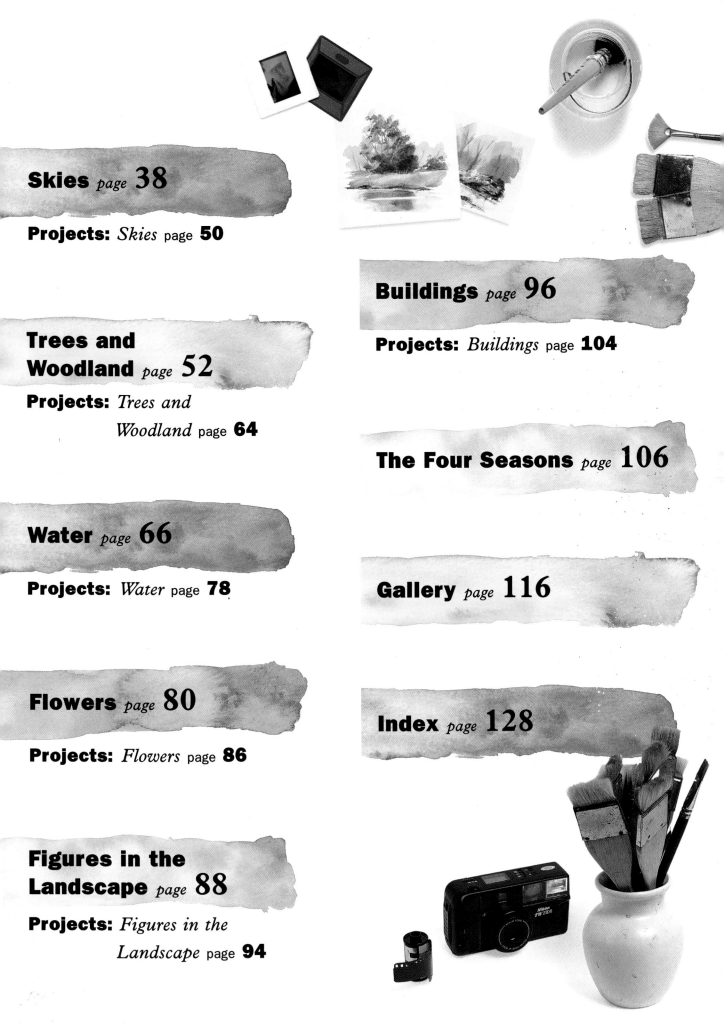

INTRODUCTION

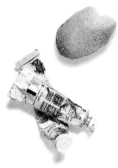

One of the most controversial topics in painting is whether or not it is acceptable to work from photographs. This subject seems to generate more words in art magazines than any other, cropping up time and time again in editorials, letters, and articles. Even in art societies it is a matter of constant debate.

USING NEW TOOLS

It seems to me that there is often an element of hypocrisy present in the "against" lobby. Doesn't it seem strange that in other fields of art, such as music, this kind of controversy appears not to exist? For example, the use of a computer in the composition of music is apparently quite acceptable. What the composer has done, in addition to using his or her musical skills, is to take the trouble to learn the use of new technology in the search for excellence. The situation is similar in art. The camera can be employed as an extra tool, a tool like any other, the best use of which has to be learned. What the "against" lobby seems to forget is that first you have to become a competent painter, skilled in all areas of your art, before you can use photography successfully as a tool. The purpose of this book is to look at the whole subject honestly and to illustrate some of the exciting possibilities that are offered by working with this extra piece of equipment. I hope that the illustrations used in this book will convince you of the validity of my conviction that photographs can be a great boon to the artist.

EXTRA SKILLS

Perhaps it will help my case if we take a quick look at some of the statements that are made against the use of the camera in watercolor painting: "It's cheating." "It's a short-cut, avoiding the need to learn drawing and sketching." "It's taking an easy option."

None of these is true. To bring a scene in a photograph to life in watercolor needs all the skill that an artist possesses. In fact, there is an *extra* skill involved, which is, of course, using your camera with competence—employing all your design skills, but this time, through a viewfinder. Any serious photographer will tell you that camera art is art in its own right. But it can also be used as an aid in the process of watercolor painting. Nevertheless, I do still feel that to produce the best paintings, an artist should first experience working outdoors, surrounded by the atmosphere and even the smells of a location, before using photography as a helpful tool.

As a teacher, I'm shown thousands of photographs each year, 75 percent of

Tumbling Water, Oregon,
14 x 11"
(35.5 x 28 cm)
The aim in this picture of an Oregon river was to create a feeling of harmony, which was achieved by keeping all the colors to one side of the color wheel. The main object of interest is the white water, which I've restricted to one fall rather than the two that existed. I've used strong directional strokes of the hake brush to impart more movement. The color at left foreground is echoed in the background trees, lending unity to the design.

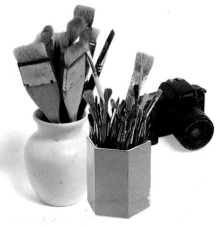

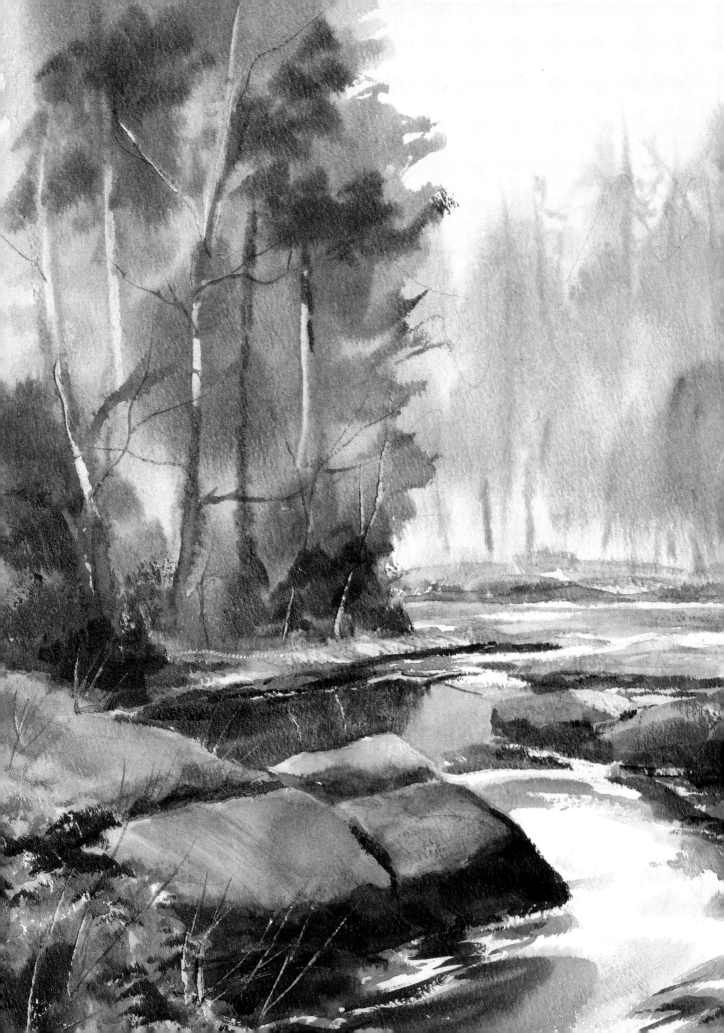

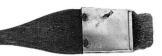

which are badly composed and uninspiring. But the worst results of painting from photographs come from the artist who attempts an exact copy of the photograph complete in every detail, warts and all, with little or no sign of the artist's own personality and flair.

THE CAMERA AS AN AID

Let us consider some examples of where the camera is most helpful. One is a crowded street scene in a city—a lively and inspiring subject, but it's almost impossible for most of us to set up our easels on a busy sidewalk or in the middle of the street. However, a quick sketch and a few good photographs will surely give you all the necessary information to compose a picture and interpret the scene in your own style back in your studio.

Another example might be a wet, misty day in the mountains. It would be extremely difficult to paint in watercolor in such weather, but equipped with a good photographic record, you'll be able to capture that interesting, overcast look in a painting at a later date. You can also photograph some of the more transient weather effects, such as a sunset that may last only a few minutes or a rainbow that could be gone in just seconds.

I am sure the stalwarts among you feel that inconvenience is a necessary part of outdoor painting. But actually, most artists are simply not always able to paint on location. Among my own friends who are professional and

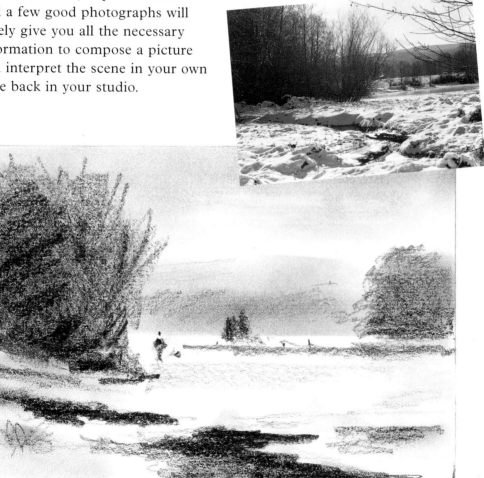

**Sun on Snow, Oregon,
12 x 16" (30 x 40.5 cm)**
*This watercolor is based on a
photograph I took in Oregon. Before
starting to paint, I made a value sketch
(opposite) in which much of the surface
of the snow has been smoothed out and
more prominence given to the
foreground stream. I reduced the mass of
trees on the left to improve the balance
of the scene, and introduced the figure
with the dog to provide a focal point.
Much of the snow is untouched white
paper. I employed only hake and rigger
brushes for this painting, using the
latter for the figure, grasses, and twigs.*

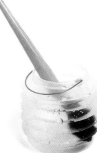

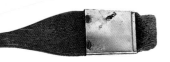

respected artists, some still prefer to work outdoors all the time, but most discovered the advantages of the camera after many years of painting in the field. The paintings of both groups are as sought after as ever, and I would defy anyone to know which were done on site and which were based on photographic reference. I still love *plein-air* painting, but I see no need to apologize for using a camera at those times when it is most advantageous to do so.

PHOTOGRAPHS AS INSPIRATION

Shortly before writing this book, I returned from a round-the-world painting and teaching trip, during which nearly all my on-site paintings were sold. However, I brought back hundreds of photographs from places as diverse as the American West, Australia, New Zealand, and Thailand. Many are pictures of subjects I had already painted on site. Looking at the photographs not only brought back with clarity the atmosphere of various locations but also inspired me to produce more watercolors as a record of my trip. They are shown often in these pages.

My own loose and impressionistic style is well suited to interpreting photographs, because my painting leaves a certain amount to the imagination of the viewer—something a photo cannot do. In fact, the entirety of information within a photograph can give a flat, static appearance to a painting. Therefore, it is the job of the artist to

bring back the excitement and mystery of a subject, and to create a relationship between artist, subject and viewer in which the viewer has to exert thought and imagination to complete the circle.

So you can see that using a camera is no easy option. First, you must learn both its potential and its limitations, and once you have taken a well-composed photograph, you will need additional skills to interpret it in a pleasing way.

PRACTICAL PROJECTS

To help you make a start at painting from photographs, I have included a number of projects in this book. Each features three photos that you can use as the basis for paintings. My own interpretations of these photographs are shown at the end of the book.

MAXIMIZING THE USE OF THE CAMERA

The intent of this book is to help you avoid the problems that are inherent to painting from photography, while maximizing the benefits of using a camera. Think of the photograph as merely a reference. You must interpret it to change the scene from one that would be static and flat as a painting to one that is filled with the qualities that attracted you to the subject in the first place. This exercise requires sensitivity, imagination, and skill, and an understanding that you have a demanding task ahead. By accepting the challenge, you will add a whole new dimension to your watercolor painting.

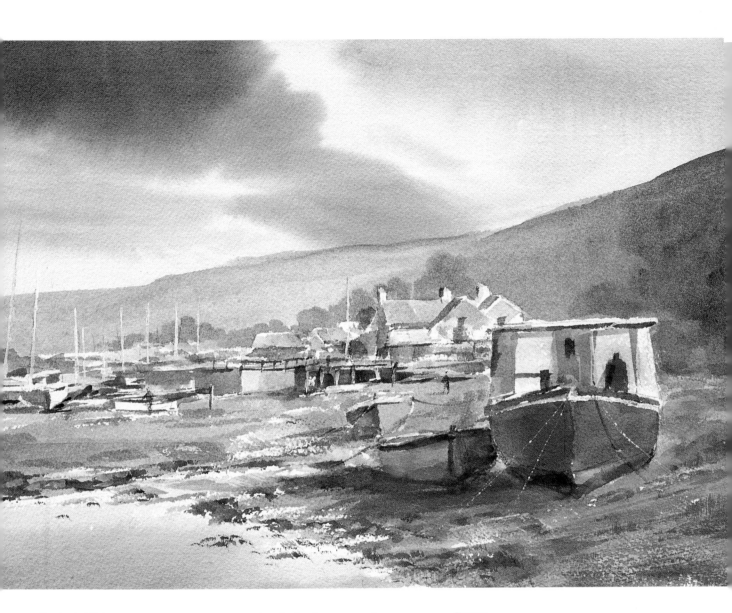

Porlock Weir,
10 x 14" (25.5 x 35.5 cm)

The photograph, taken in Devon, England, is slightly weight-heavy on the right-hand side. I corrected it in my painting by creating a rich cloud formation top left to provide balance. I've repeated many touches of color throughout—even the red of the gas cylinder on the foreground boat deck is repeated in the group of boats on the left. I omitted the house at the right edge, finding it an unnecessary distraction. Also note the variety of color in the foreground at right, and the use of dry brush for pebbles at the water's edge. I've simplified and altered some background buildings, and used gouache to describe the boats' white masts. I've also faintly suggested a couple of figures to complete this friendly scene.

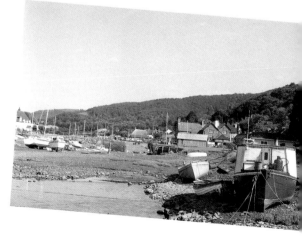

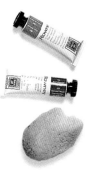

The equipment required to paint watercolors from photographs need not be costly. An inexpensive camera will supply you with color prints from which to make value sketches. You can then draw an image on watercolor paper before beginning to paint. If you employ this method, first draw on tracing paper and make your corrections there, instead of later, on your watercolor paper, where you would mar its surface by erasing. Go over your drawing on the back of the tracing paper with a soft pencil, then transfer the image by pressing it onto your watercolor paper. Other transfer methods are shown later in this chapter.

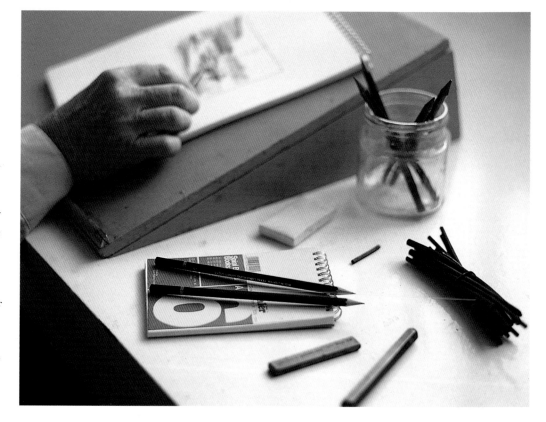

My sketching materials include soft pencils, graphite sticks, graphite pencils, and sticks of charcoal. A ring-bound sketchbook and a kneaded eraser complete the kit.

SKETCHING MATERIALS

The pencils you use for making a value sketch must be soft—from 2B to 6B. Flat graphite sticks and solid graphite pencils are very good, as they will prohibit you from putting in too much unnecessary detail, and flat sides also produce areas of tone more quickly. Sticks of charcoal are an alternative, but they are fragile and smudge easily. Make your sketch on a pad of ordinary sketch paper—watercolor paper is not suitable, unless you want to do your value sketches in watercolor as I sometimes do, using burnt umber or Payne's gray. A kneaded eraser will also be useful to pick out the whites.

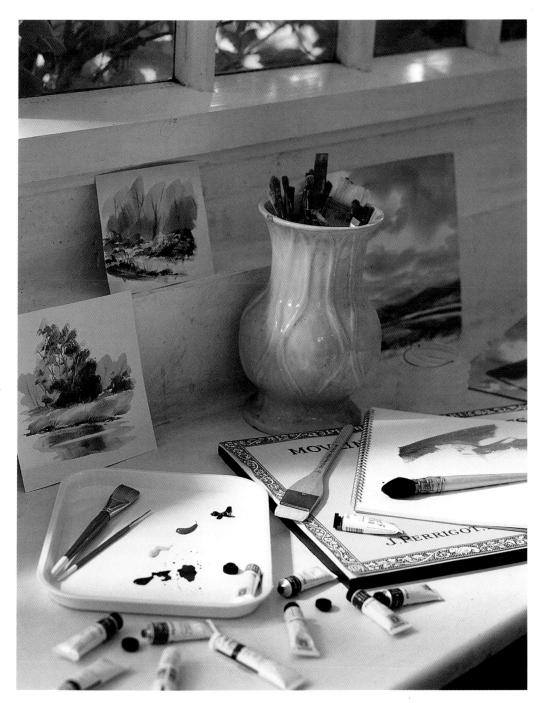

Here you can see my four brushes: the 1½" (38 mm) hake, the 1" (25 mm) flat, the # 3 rigger, and the oval mop. My seven favorite colors are: lemon yellow, raw sienna, burnt umber, alizarin crimson, light red, French ultramarine, and Payne's gray.

WATERCOLOR MATERIALS

While you may use whichever brushes suit you, I like large brushes best, as they prevent the precise copying of photographs. The only small brush I use is the rigger; it's great for fine details. Everything else is done with a flat, a hake (pronounced hah-kay), and a mop brush—brushes that prevent belaboring details.

Color range is a matter of choice. I prefer to work from a limited palette, using large tubes of paint and a big plastic tray to mix them on. Most of my painting is done on pads of watercolor paper or blocks of Arches Cold Pressed.

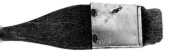

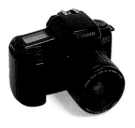

A corner of my studio, showing some of my photographic equipment and my slide projector.

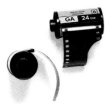

CAMERAS

My view is that a camera should be simple to use and light to carry. The one I use most is a single lens reflex (SLR) camera. Most are automatic and do nearly all the work for you, except, of course, for the composing—of which more later. I also have two extra lenses—a wide-angle lens that reduces scale and widens the field of vision, and a zoom lens to bring distant objects nearer. You may also find a tripod useful for low light levels when the shutter speed drops below an acceptable figure for hand-held photography.

You do not need to spend a lot of money on a camera; most produce quite acceptable results, and a good photograph depends more upon the artistry of the photographer than the quality of the equipment.

TRANSFERRING THE IMAGE

Transparencies are usually on 35mm film, so they will need to be enlarged. One way to enlarge is by putting them in a projector focused on a light wall in a darkened room. The image can then be drawn on white paper. The size of the enlargement will depend upon the distance of the projector from the wall. Alternatively, you can have excellent prints made from your transparencies by laser copier, a service available at photoprocessing and/or photocopy shops.

PRINTS

The simplest and best method of using a print is to hold it in your left hand while you draw with your right. This isn't always as easy as it sounds, especially if the scene is a complex one; whatever else you're going to do with the scene, your drawing is obviously going to be an enlarged version of it, incorporating all your compositional changes.

The traditional way to establish the correct proportions is to place your photo in a corner of the paper, joining the opposite corner with a diagonal line and extending this line onto the paper. The proportions of the enlargement will be correct if the corner is placed at any point along the diagonal line.

Another method is to photocopy the print, enlarging it to the required size. This can be used as a guide to making your drawing on cartridge paper. You'll then need a sheet of transfer paper, which can be bought at most art shops. This is thin tissue, coated on one side with graphite. Failing this, you could simply rub soft pencil over the back of your drawing, then trace through onto the

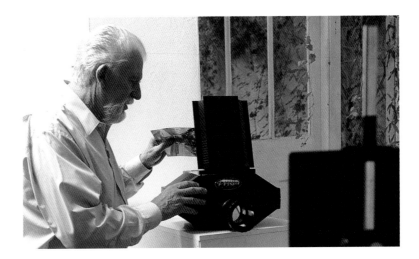

watercolor paper with a ballpoint pen. This will save making too many alterations on the watercolor paper. A third alternative is to use one of the projectors on the market that will enlarge the print for you.

However, with all these aids there comes the temptation to produce tight, overworked drawings that could then reflect in your finished painting, especially in such subjects as flowers, foliage, and skies. Like the photographs, such equipment must be your servant and not your master. Try constantly to improve your skills in freehand drawing, and as you progress you may find you only need to use special equipment as a time-saver on occasions when you are producing really complex subjects. Never use equipment of this kind as a crutch in order to avoid learning to draw. After all, virtually every photograph needs considerable alteration if you're to create a personalized painting.

A horizontal image projector can enlarge an original print up to twenty times its size.

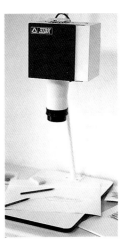

An overhead projector is another option for working with prints.

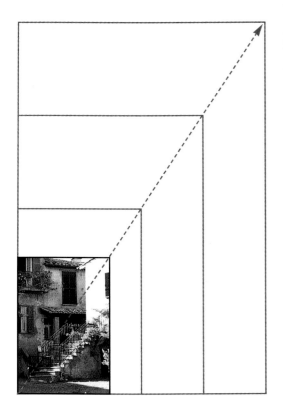

The traditional way of scaling up a photograph is to put it in one corner of the paper and then draw a diagonal line to the opposite corner.

COMPOSING YOUR PHOTOGRAPHS

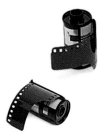

The photographs you use for reference in your watercolor paintings need to be the best you can obtain, so in this chapter we are going to look at ways to improve your photography. It's a sad fact that many photos taken today, even with all the technical help available from modern cameras, are simply no use at all as reference for paintings. The missing ingredient is composition. Even highly skilled watercolorists who regularly practice the principles of composition in their paintings don't seem to be able to relate them to photography, while in any twenty prints shown to me by my students, perhaps only two or three will be suitable for use as reference material. A good, well-composed photograph will make you want to reach for your brushes.

THE BASIC RULES

Perhaps the most basic rule is simply this: Always try to have three planes in your photograph—foreground, middle distance, and far distance. Look at the same view from different angles. What may appear breathtaking seen from the top of a hill may be boring as a printed photograph. While the middle and far distance are usually in evidence, a suitable foreground object is often missing. Be patient and move around until you find one that satisfies you—

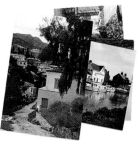

it may be a tree, a gate, or even a gatepost. Look through your viewfinder and make sure that you have all three planes in view; if you haven't, don't press the shutter.

For example, you might be considering a beach scene with two boats of similar size. What you need to avoid here is taking the shot with the boats at either side of your photograph. Instead, move around until your viewfinder shows you a picture in which one boat dominates in the foreground (the scene could be even more interesting if the boats overlap). If you're photographing a wooded area, rather than just taking a general view, find a position where you have one tree, perhaps of a different species from the mass, prominent in the foreground.

PROVIDING A LEAD-IN

Try to find a feature that will lead the viewer's eye into your photograph—a footpath, a cart track, or a stream. Look for interesting close-ups, and remember that you don't always need bright sunshine; misty and cloudy conditions can sometimes be more interesting. Try the view both horizontally and vertically. Practice without a film in your camera, concentrating entirely on composing what you see through your viewfinder. An hour or two spent in this way will be invaluable, and you'll soon begin to understand the difference

Waterfall Near Glencoe (detail)
This loose interpretation is from a photograph I took in Scotland. It is painted very much wet-into-wet, yet at the same time I tried to put in as much rich, powerful color as I could—hence the almost purple rocks in the foreground. There is a very strong but simple pattern here, with the most contrast being confined to foreground water and rocks.

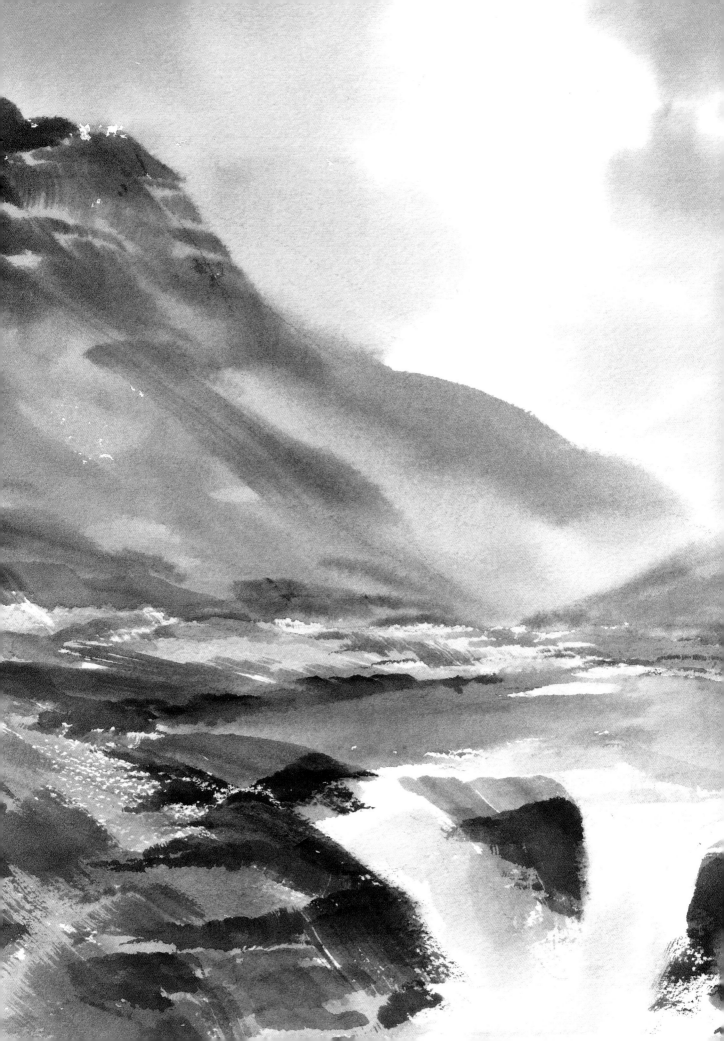

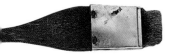

between a good composition and a poor one.

No matter how much time you spend photographing, chances are that once you have had your prints processed, you will need to do some careful editing. Look at each print critically, considering the tonal values, the depth of field, and whether there are conflicting centers of interest, with too many objects all vying for your attention.

A good way to assess your prints is to take two L-shaped pieces of paper, overlap them to make a picture shape, and then move them around until you are focusing on the heart of the scene. You will probably find that you are looking at the very thing that attracted you to that particular view in the first place. Quite often, a photograph with which you are initially disappointed will look far more interesting once all the clutter is removed. A horizontal may become a vertical, or a boat that was facing out of the photo may face inward with judicial manipulation of your L-shapes.

Many of the skills involved in photography and painting are so closely linked as to be interchangeable. Becoming a good photographer will improve your painting, and vice versa. So much depends on good design and composition—and this principle applies equally to photography and painting.

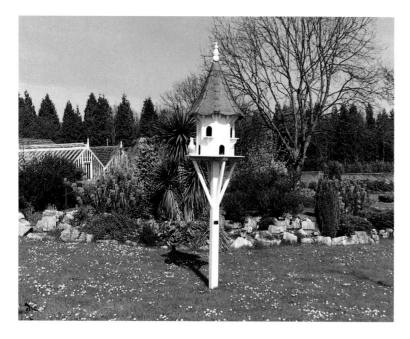

▲ *Here the main object of interest, the birdhouse, is right in the center—possibly one of the worst compositional faults. This stricture applies to any focus of interest, whether it be a boat, house, bridge, person, or animal.*

▶ *In this photograph, the birdhouse has been moved to one side, immediately making the composition more satisfying.*

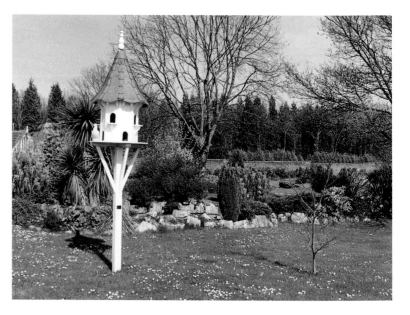

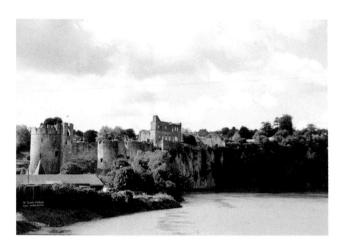

◄ *This is a conventional view of Chepstow Castle in Wales. It could be used as the basis for a painting, but would need a lot of preparatory work in a value sketch. The sky and the river are much too bland, and the whole scene is lacking in drama.*

► *Another approach is shown here, using a foreground boat and bank. This view hasn't quite worked as a composition, however, because the boat and the castle compete with each other.*

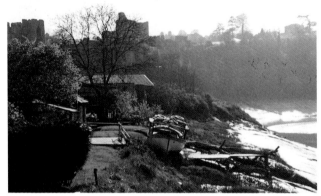

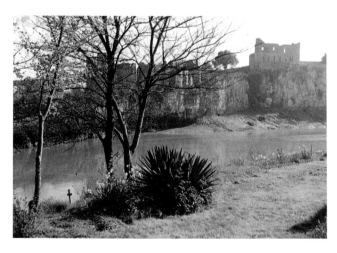

◄ *This photograph introduces a vertical element into the picture, linking the two banks of the river, but the foreground foliage is too dominant, blocking the entrance into the picture.*

► *This view of the castle is very satisfying. The strong vertical element of the tree in the foreground balances the castle wall and takes the eye directly toward it.*

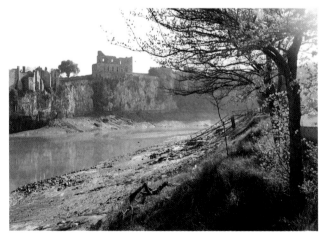

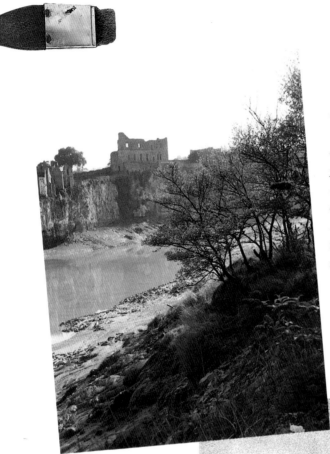

◀ *Finally, I decided to use this portrait photo as the basis for my painting. I decided that this framing of the shot made the castle's massive bulk look more dramatic.*

***Chepstow Castle, 16 x 12"
(40.5 x 30 cm)***
In my painting, I aimed to get a much greater variation in color than was apparent in my photograph. I lightened the river to make the tonal value more distinct from that of the foreground bank, and warmed up the scene with pinks and mauves. I also painted in a more interesting sky, interspersing blue with paper-white clouds.

▶ *I thought that this photograph was bottom-heavy, so in my value sketch, I discarded part of the foreground and enlarged the sky. I also moved the tree mass slightly to the right to avoid masking the castle.*

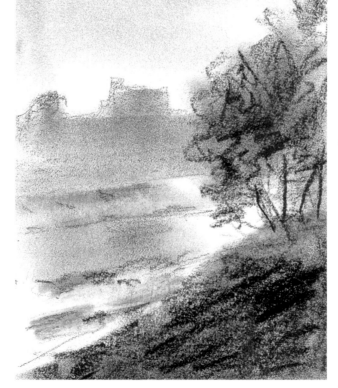

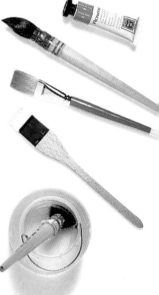

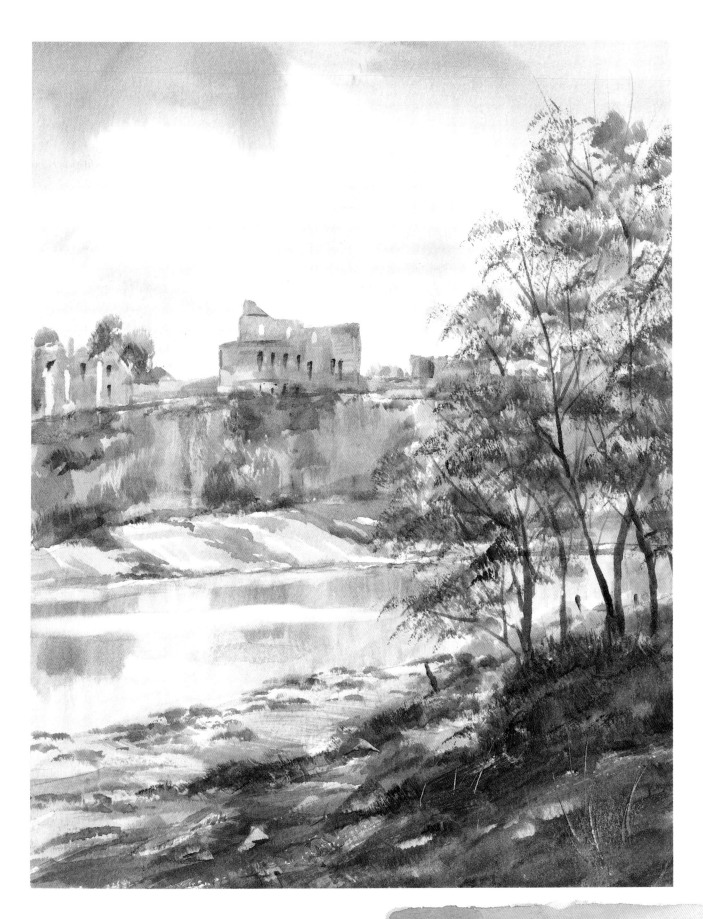

COMPOSITION AND DESIGN

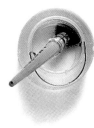

Once you have followed the advice in the previous chapter, you will be producing photographs that are reasonably well balanced, containing a main object of interest, and encompassing foreground, middle distance, and far distance. Then you will be at a good starting point—and should be itching to paint, to capture those vital elements that stopped you in your tracks in the first place. Before you can convert a photograph into a painting of lasting worth, however, there is a lot more work to do.

COMPOSING YOUR PAINTING

The previous chapter discussed the composition of your photograph, but even the most perfectly composed photograph will not translate directly into a well-composed painting. Composing through a viewfinder and composing a finished painting on paper are by the very nature of things slightly different exercises.

For example, although your photograph will have a main object of interest, it may be necessary to change a path, a road, or the sweep of a river to take the viewer's eye into the picture and on to the center of interest. There may be a boat or a figure facing out of the picture which will need to be reversed or moved to prevent the viewer's eye from straying rather than remaining captured within the scene. Foreground walls or fences in your photograph may require removal or opening up—after all, you don't want to fence your viewer out! The composition may be vastly improved by adding a foreground shadow that is not on the photograph; on the other hand, some shadows may need to be lightened and made more transparent. Always avoid placing the horizon in the center of your painting, as this will cut the picture in half. Think carefully too about the positioning of the center of interest, which should be a different distance from each edge of the painting.

THE PRINCIPLES OF DESIGN

More specific rules for composition can be defined by considering the principles of design. These are not complicated and, in fact, most are just common sense, but they will improve your work dramatically. Your knowledge or ignorance of them will be evidenced in every painting you produce.

There are only eight principles of design to memorize, and they are: contrast, dominance, unity, gradation, balance, harmony, variation, and alternation. It is easy enough to learn this list by heart; the difficult part is applying the principles to each painting. It is not necessarily possible to apply every rule to every painting, but the more you can put each into practice, the better your painting will be.

***Grounded,**
14 x 11"
(35.5 x 28 cm)
For the last thirteen years, I've been running workshops in a tiny lobster-fishing village on the coast of Maine. This harbor scene has one of the lobster boats as its main object of interest, so I have placed it at a different distance from each edge of the paper, making it stand out by darkening the area immediately around it. Also notice that the boat is not challenged by anything else in the picture that might distract the viewer's eye.*

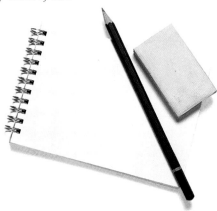

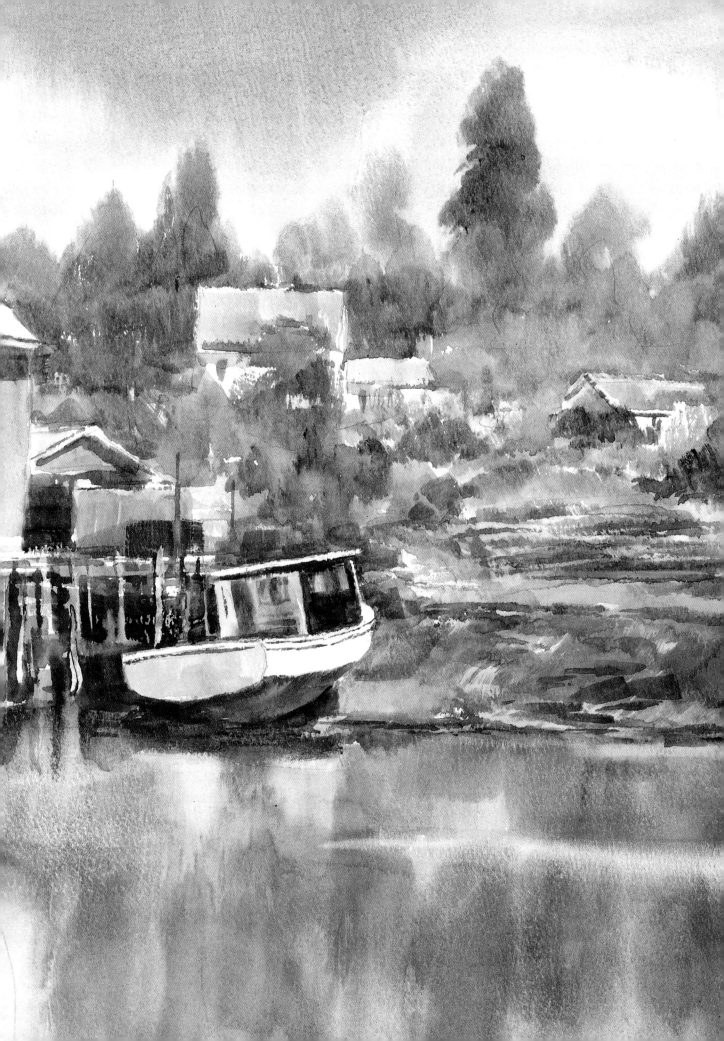

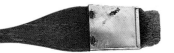

CONTRAST

Contrast is an abrupt change from one state to another: warm to cool, light to dark, hard to soft. When working with photographs, you will often find that you have to increase contrast in areas to which you want to attract the eye, and decrease contrast in less important areas.

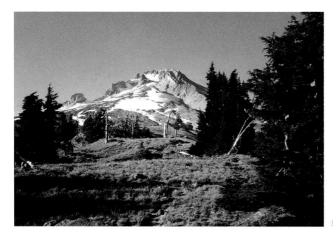

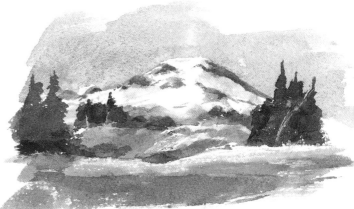

Above, patches of white snow provide good contrast with dark trees, and the hard outline of the mountain contrasts with the softer texture of trees and grass. The thin white tree trunks provide added contrast.

The contrast between snow and trees was sufficiently strong for me to be able to lighten the green somewhat in this watercolor. However, I have darkened some of the rock face to provide stronger contrast with the white of the snow.

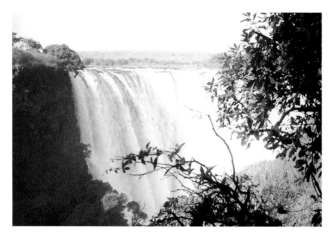

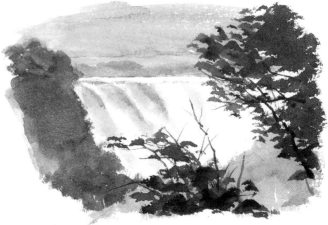

I took this photograph because I wanted to record dark, clean-edged foliage against the soft white foam of the falls. The color contrast is good, too, with light grass showing up well against dark twigs and leaves.

When it came to painting the scene, I decided to lighten the foliage on the right and on the side of the falls to the left to give more harmony of color, but there is still plenty of contrast between the white foam and surrounding vegetation.

DOMINANCE

I believe that this is the most important principle of all. The term *dominance* means that in any painting, one object must be more important than all others. You can make that object larger, brighter, the area of greatest contrast, or even a combination of such elements. If a dominant feature is not evident in your photograph, be sure to provide it in your value sketch. For example, if you have three mountain peaks or three clouds of the same size, you should make some changes to give one dominance.

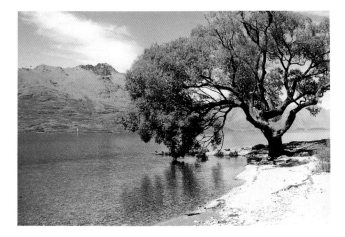

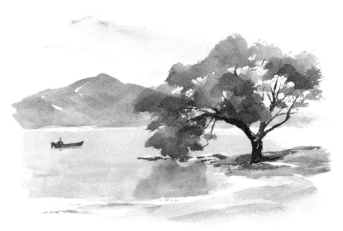

This photograph was taken at an angle that gave the foreground tree dominance over the mountains. In fact, the tree is perhaps too dominant, leaving the rest of the scene as just a backdrop.

In the painting, I added a small boat to correct the imbalance of the photograph. The sweep of the beach and rocks lead the viewer's eye into the picture and to the boat.

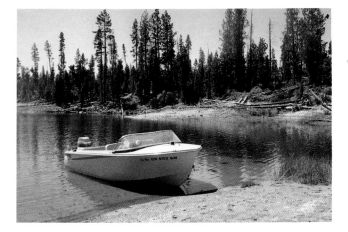

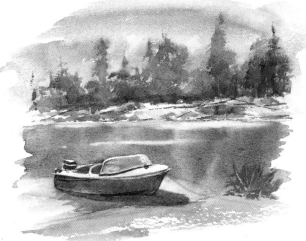

There can be no doubt at all about the dominant object here; the boat is a manmade object, which always draws the eye. The rest of the picture acts simply as a background for the boat.

I needed to change the design little for the painting, other than to broaden the stretch of water showing behind the boat in order to bring more depth of field into the scene.

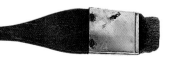

UNITY

Unity is an interlocking of all the elements in a painting. While your photograph may show a collection of disparate objects, as is often the nature of things, your job as an artist is to unite these elements in your value sketch, before you start your painting. Overlapping is useful here, or you could echo shapes or colors. Have a close look at the illustrations here and see how I have used this principle.

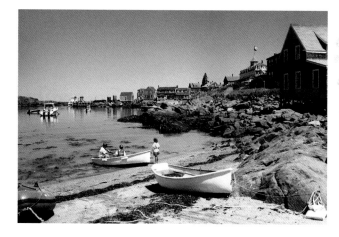

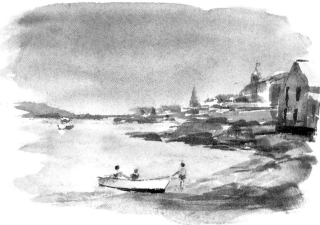

This was an attractive scene to photograph but it had too many scattered objects in it—the viewer's eye is distracted by disparate shapes and colors.

I created unity in my painting by removing some objects and concentrating on a single boat. The sweep of beach is a good unifying factor, as is the echoing of the life jacket's yellow elsewhere in the picture.

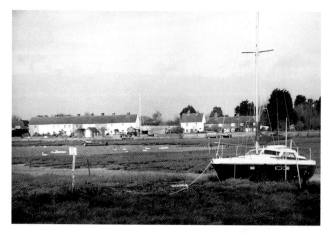

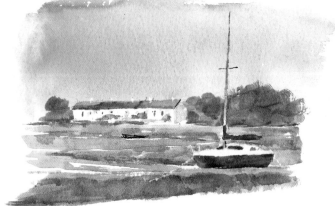

There are plenty of soft brown and ochre colors in the grasses, foliage, and house rooftops in this photograph to provide unity of color. The white of the small sailing boat is also echoed in the white row of houses.

Repeating the whites worked well here, and I also included white in the water for emphasis. The mast is a useful unifying factor linking earth to sky. The colors in the roofs are echoed in the foreground grasses, as is the sky color in the water.

GRADATION

This technique is employed to enliven a flat area. It is the gradual change from one state to another: light to dark or cool to warm. Photographs often lack this quality, especially in the foreground, and in this case, it's probably better to ignore the picture and put in your own graded wash. This technique is often needed in the portrayal of a row of buildings, where making changes in the wall surfaces will overcome a flat, dull appearance.

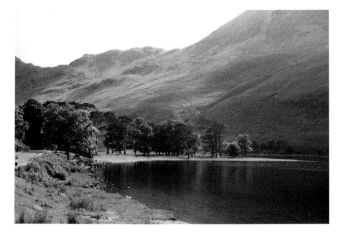

This photograph shows a rather solid bank of flat greens in the background trees, and the expanse of water is somewhat monotonous.

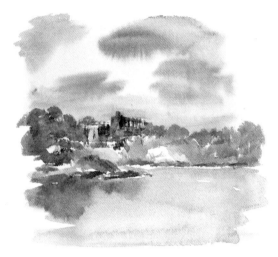

For my painting I graded the tree greens and the browns and grays in the water to add interest to what could otherwise be a dull painting.

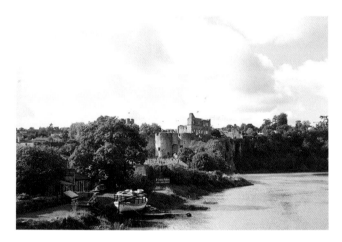

The subtle tones of mountains of the English Lake District reflected in water make a pleasing photograph, but if they were translated directly into a painting, would lack depth and interest.

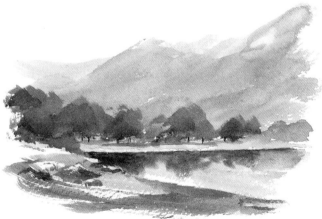

Here, I use a gradation of greens from cool to warm as they come forward, repeating those values in the reflections. Also notice value gradation in the trees from dark to light, as well as in the colors of the foreground shore.

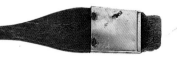

BALANCE

Balance is an important element in a composition. Any large object in a scene has a tendency to unbalance it, but this can be corrected by moving it nearer to the center and balancing it with a smaller object farther away on the other side. Think of a seesaw: If you have a heavy weight on one side of the seesaw, it can be balanced by a lighter weight farther away from the center. While you could have equal weights on both sides, this would be far less interesting visually.

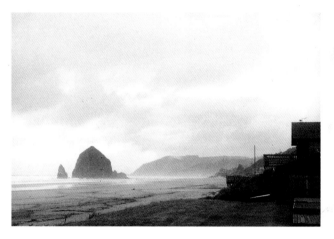

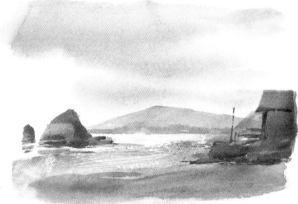

When I took this photograph, I aimed to balance the vertical bulk of a large rock just offshore with the horizontal expanse of sandy beach nearer to the camera.

Nevertheless, the painting is about the rock, so I have made it a more dominant feature by contrasting it against a lighter sea and sky than appear in the photograph.

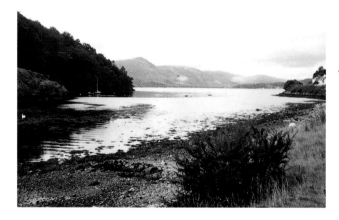

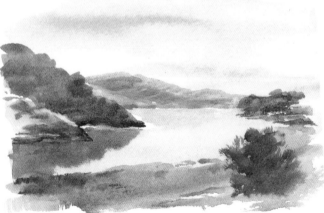

I framed this photo so that the dark foreground bush foliage would balance the heavy shape of the promontory on the left side of the picture.

The bush in the photograph almost disappears into the beach, so I've corrected it by changing the tone of the beach and contrasting the top of the bush against light water.

HARMONY

Harmonious colors are those adjacent to each other on the color wheel, such as orange and red on the warm side and blue and green on the cool. Harmonious shapes are squares and rectangles or circles and ovals. If these elements are lacking in your photograph, you will need to create them in your finished painting.

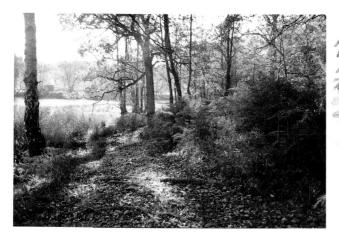

Autumn colors often provide their own natural harmony in a scene, as is the case in the photograph above. The soft browns, rusts, and ochres of dying foliage blend harmoniously with the darker tones of the tree trunks.

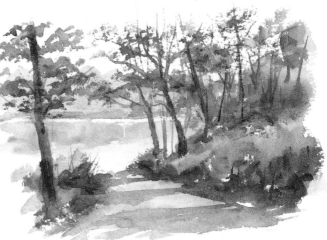

Distant woodland looks very appealing when painted in a variety of soft, cool mauves, which complement the warmth of browns and oranges used in the foreground and impart depth to the whole painting.

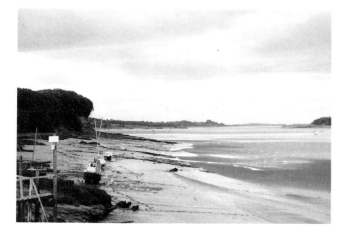

In estuary scenes like this, wet sand reflects the sky color, giving its own sense of harmony to the scene. If the presence of brightly colored boats mars the effect, you can simply change their color in your painting.

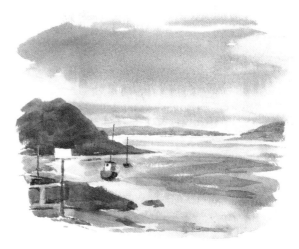

In my painting, to emphasize the existing harmony between sand and sky, I use a very restricted palette and apply the color for sand with directional brushstrokes to echo the shape of the cloud.

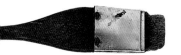

VARIATION

Although repetition may be employed in a painting to great effect, it must be used with variation to avoid monotony. Try to provide variety in repeated shapes or colors. A uniform row of trees in a photo can be modified in the value sketch by varying tree sizes, angles, and the distances between them.

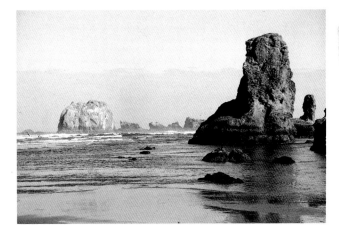

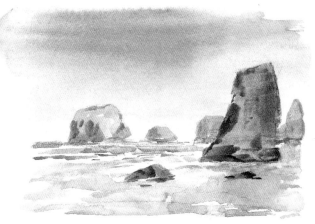

This photograph reveals a good deal of repetition in waves and the shapes and colors of rocks. Copied exactly, this would fail as a painting.

Although repetition can be effective in a painting, it must always be done with variation. The rocks here are more varied in color, tone, size, and spacing than in the photograph.

ALTERNATION

The principle of alternation is most usually applied to color—placing intense color to alternate with neutrals, or warm colors with cool ones.

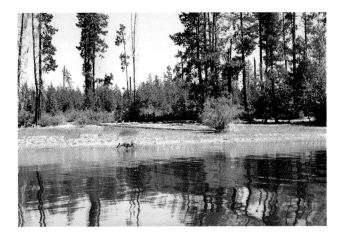

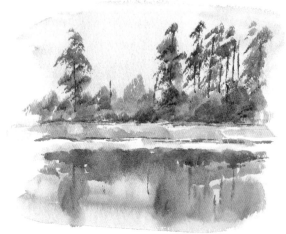

What attracted me to this scene was the reflection of vegetation and sky in the water. In this photograph there already exists alternation of warm and cool colors.

I accentuated the alternation somewhat in my painting, in which warm and cool colors have been alternated from top to bottom and from left to right to avoid monotony.

APPLYING THE PRINCIPLES

It is neither practical nor necessary to include every principle in every painting, but you should habitually test each of your finished paintings against the list of principles to make sure you have not ignored them. It will take time to absorb the principles so completely that you will automatically incorporate them in your painting, so you may find it useful initially to have the list of principles pinned to your board to jog your memory.

In my advanced classes, I start by teaching these basic principles, after which we critique the paintings brought along by each student, judging them strictly by the principles of design. This operation is a real eye-opener. Everyone can see ways in which their paintings could have been improved had they applied the design principles. From then on, the students' work progresses by leaps and bounds as they learn to use this critical yardstick.

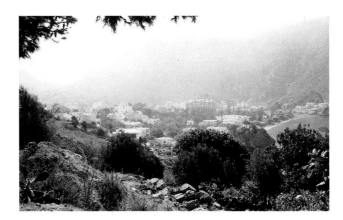

▲ *Including overhanging foliage in the very front of a photograph is a classic way of adding interest and depth, but it does not necessarily translate successfully into a painting. This view of a village is rather spoiled by bushes blocking the nearest part of it, and they also distract the viewer's attention. Consequently, this picture needs some adjustment of composition before it will work well as a painting.*

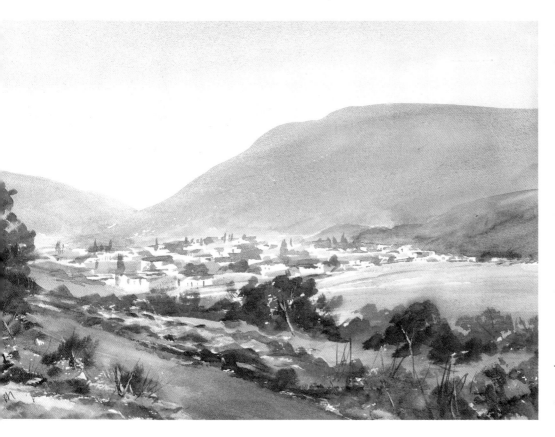

Village on Kalymnos
11¼ x 15½"
(28.5 x 39.5 cm)
The center of interest is the village on this Greek island, rendered with contrasting patches of white and color. I used graded washes on the hills and sky. The eye is taken into the picture by the path and led to the tree on the left, which is balanced by strong foreground color on the right. Unity is given by repeating the pinks.

THE VALUE SKETCH

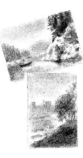

Whether you are painting from photographs or from life, your work begins long before you pick up a brush. A major part of this vitally important "thinking period" is your value sketch.

This is the message that I give to my students at the beginning of each course. They all agree with the wisdom of this approach, but a couple of hours later, for some inexplicable reason, most students ignore the whole concept—even though they know that most professional artists begin a painting by working out its values in a value sketch. Once I have persuaded my students to produce their value sketches, I find them attempting to put in every detail, having forgotten that the object of the exercise is to reduce the subject to a simple pattern of lights and darks, which probably differs from the original view.

VALUES

Let us assume that you have never before attempted a value sketch. The first thing you need to understand is that value is simply the darkness or lightness of a color. Any painting, no matter how colorful or subdued, consists of various values that form a basic pattern. Tony Couch, a well-known American painter whose work I admire, has said, "I recall reading and hearing about 'tonal values' for years without understanding how to use them. When one day I discovered

they are placed in a pattern, it was as if the sun had just risen: my paintings improved a thousand percent." The stronger the pattern is, the more arresting the painting will be, and the time to establish your pattern is in your value sketch.

MAKING A VALUE SKETCH

If you are using pencil, get into the habit of varying the amount of pressure, producing different values from each grade of pencil. Think of a scale from one to ten, with the pure white of the paper being one and solid black being ten. Once you begin to paint, to achieve ten, you will need almost pure paint with hardly any water at all, while one on the scale will remain untouched paper. Your sketch pad does not need to be very big, as your value sketch should be only about 4 × 3" (10 × 7.5 cm), but it must be on smooth paper.

Before you start on your first value sketch, spend some time doodling on cheap paper with various pencils. As with anything else, you need to be at ease with your materials. Once you accept the concept of value sketches and have had a bit of practice, you will find that you'll enjoy them in their own right. Take half a dozen photographs and do value sketches of them, even if you aren't going to take them any further.

That is the accepted way of producing a value sketch, but my favorite method is a little different. I use

Fjord in Lofoten (detail)

This painting is based on a photograph taken on a trip up the coast of Norway. The far-distant mountain is just one thin wash, but as I moved forward in the picture, I introduced more and more texture and color. The foreground rocks were produced by scraping the paint with the edge of a credit card. There is a mixture of warm and cool color in the mountain on the right, which adds to the general interest of the painting.

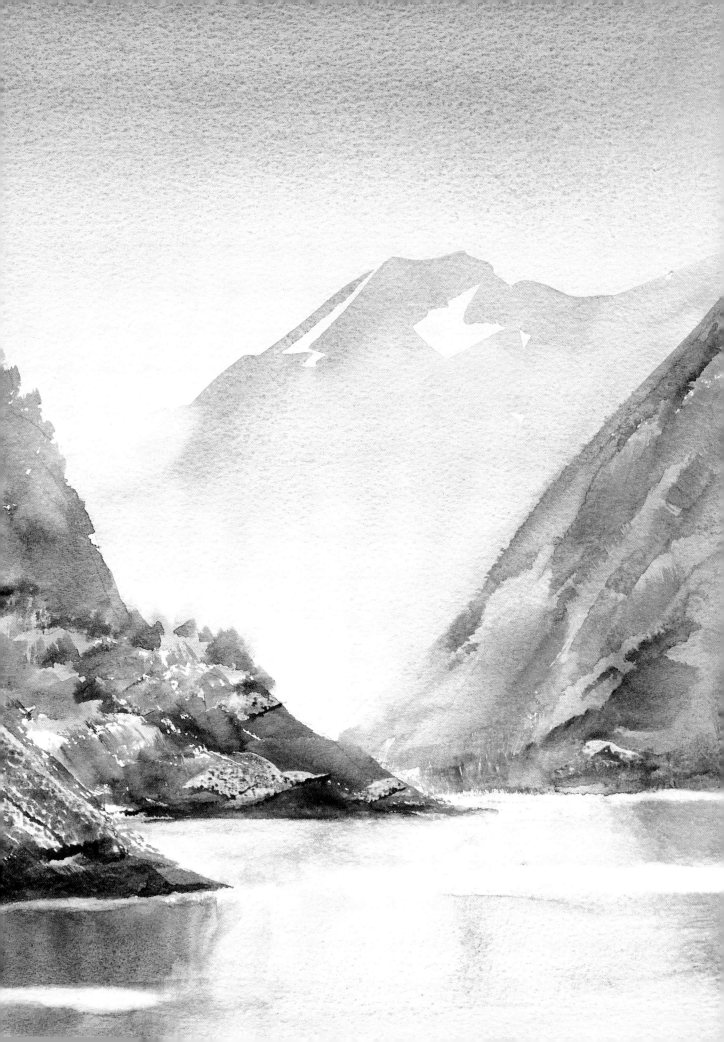

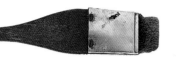

This is a typical example of a value sketch drawn with a soft pencil. The soft tone of the sky was put in by employing a smudging technique with the index finger, using a piece of white paper as a mask. In the original photograph, the value of the tree and the bridge were too similar and the river was dry.

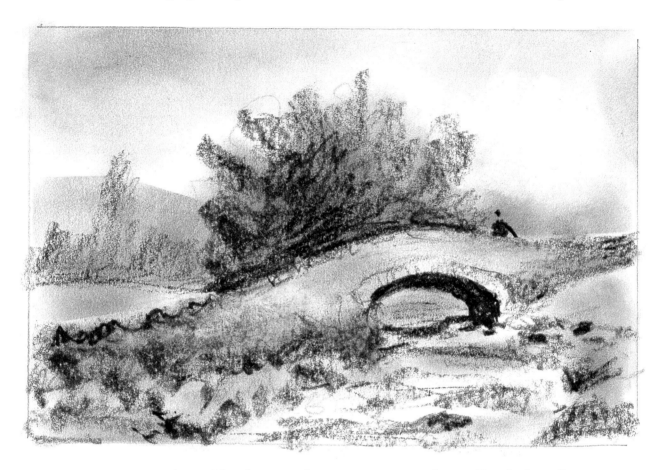

watercolor—either burnt umber or Payne's gray—on scraps of watercolor paper. As with pencil sketches, my value sketches are kept to a maximum of 4 x 3" (10 x 7.5 cm), and I scale values in exactly the same way. The only brushes I use are a hake and a 1" (25 mm) flat, perhaps bringing in my rigger for a figure.

Whichever method you use, avoid putting in any detail whatsoever, concentrating instead on producing a pattern of lights and darks in miniature. Don't think of the components of your subject as individual objects; see them only as areas of tone. Don't draw lines around anything. They are not only unnecessary; they have no place in a value sketch. Confine white areas of a value sketch to those parts of the final painting that will be left as untouched white paper. Every other area should have some tone on it.

As value is a darkness or lightness of any color, if you paint a red house against a green tree and the two colors are similar in value, the effect is flat. What you need is to make the tree a darker green or the house a lighter red so that the painting will have a range of values. Exaggerate

This value sketch is done in watercolor in Payne's gray. Notice the different values obtained by using different strengths of paint. The rocks were produced by scraping with a piece of credit card while the wash was still damp.

darks and lights. Put two on your scale against eight, or even one against ten. Remember that you are aiming to produce your subject as a pattern of lights and darks.

AVOIDING PROBLEMS

The most common problems associated with value sketches include:

1. Not enough thought. A quote from the late Ed Whitney, one of America's best-known teachers of watercolor, is useful here: "Design like a tortoise; paint like a hare."

2. Being in too much of a rush—don't neglect that valuable planning or thinking time before you make a mark on the paper.

3. Believing that it's possible to solve all the problems in the final painting; regard your value sketch as an architect would his plan for a new building—it must be right!

4. Failure to follow the value sketch in the final painting; keep the sketch pinned above your painting and refer to it constantly. This way you will avoid producing a painting that is a weakened version of what was originally a strong design.

Once you are able to produce good value sketches, you will see a marked improvement in your finished painting. By learning to contrast areas of tone, you will produce paintings with more sparkle and excitement than you would ever have thought possible.

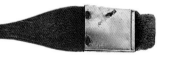

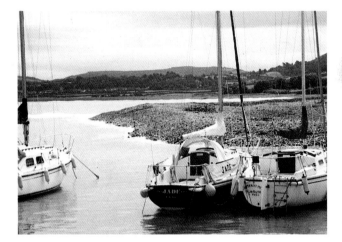

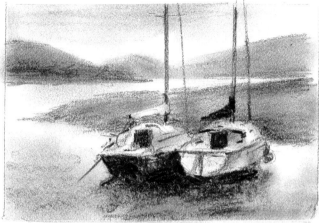

In this photograph of Porlock Weir, the third boat half out of the frame seemed awkward and superfluous. I also thought the hills were too flat.

Here I've darkened the hill on the left to balance the boats, then dropped the level of the beach behind the boats for counterbalance. The boats have also been moved slightly toward the center.

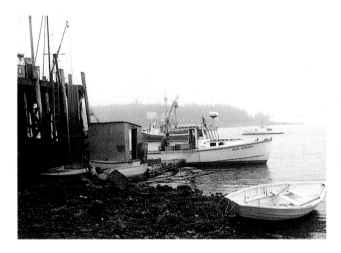

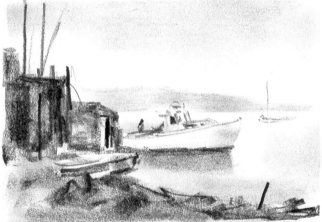

The two foreground boats compete for the viewer's attention in this misty scene in Maine. Also, the rowboat points out of the picture.

In my value sketch I removed the rowboat and the middle-distance boats, adjusted the rocks, and added a distant yacht to help balance the picture.

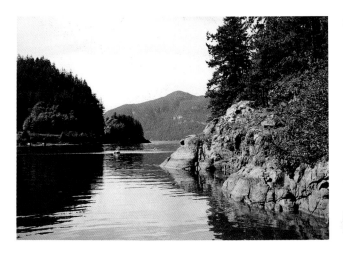

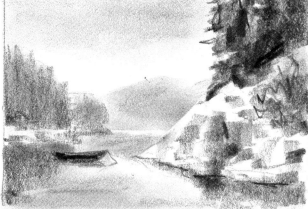

The trees on the left in this Canadian scene were too dark, attracting the viewer's attention too much. I wanted the trees and rocks on the right to be the dominant feature.

In my value sketch I've increased the contrast between trees and rocks, weakened the trees on the left, and added a moored boat to provide a main object of interest. Notice how the foreground rocks point to the boat, which in turn balances the trees on the right.

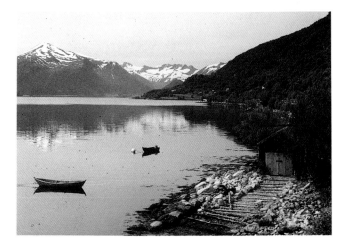

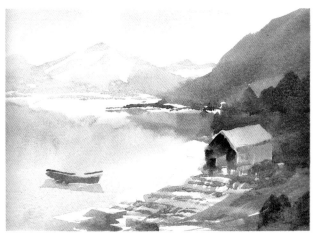

In this Norwegian landscape, the boathouse on the right is almost obscured by foliage. It is also dark in tone. The viewer's interest is caught first by the boats and then the snowcapped mountains.

In my watercolor sketch, I've made the boathouse the main object of interest, and have also given more depth to the picture by lightening and cooling the distant mountains.

SKIES

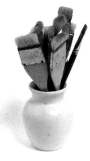

When I drive around the countryside, I'm always on the lookout for interesting cloud formations and different color combinations in the sky. I try to have my camera with me at all times, but naturally, the best skies appear when I've left my camera at home. Sky conditions and colors change so quickly that they surely strengthen the argument for using the camera as a tool in painting. For example, you can photograph a racing sky on a wild and windy day that would flatten your easel in seconds, or in pouring rain that would instantly ruin a watercolor painting.

It's not necessary to look for a perfect landscape condition when taking a sky photograph. The landscape below will usually be too dark, because the camera's light meter reacts to the light in the sky. Conversely, in a landscape photograph, the sky often appears almost white, because the camera has judged the light needed for the landscape rather than the sky—hence the need for separate photographs as reference for skies. Aim for a good selection of skies that you can use with any subject you want to paint.

TRANSFERRING SKIES INTO PAINT

The rule about never attempting to copy exactly from your photos must be applied even more strictly when you are using a photographic reference for a sky. Your picture is intended to be simply a visual reminder of what the sky condition was like. Often you may use only a section of the sky, perhaps providing balance in your picture by making a dominant cloud provide weight on the other side of the painting from a feature in the landscape.

Although I have painted hundreds of skies and can perfectly well produce one out of my head when necessary, I find that looking at a photograph out of the corner of my eye keeps the sky more relevant and authentic. However, anyone looking at the photograph and the painting would probably not see any resemblance between the two.

An important point to remember is that you don't want your sky and foreground to compete, but rather to complement each other. For instance, with a low, simple horizon, you can really go to town on producing wild, chaotic skies, leaving the foreground completely uncluttered. Conversely, if your subject is a complex street scene or marketplace, your sky will need to be restrained; otherwise, the two areas of the picture will conflict.

UNITY WITH THE LAND

To give unity to the whole painting, the sky color should be repeated in the foreground. This is particularly important where your subject includes water, even if it is just a puddle. If you are using two separate photographs to build up a picture, you need to be careful that the

Low Tide on the Severn,
14 x 12"
(35.5 x 30 cm)
In this Severn Estuary scene near my home in England, there is good contrast between the soft clouds and the strong textural feel to the foreground. One unifying factor is provided by the repetition of the cloud color in the water; another is the foreground tree that links the earth to the sky.

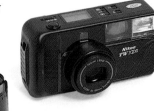

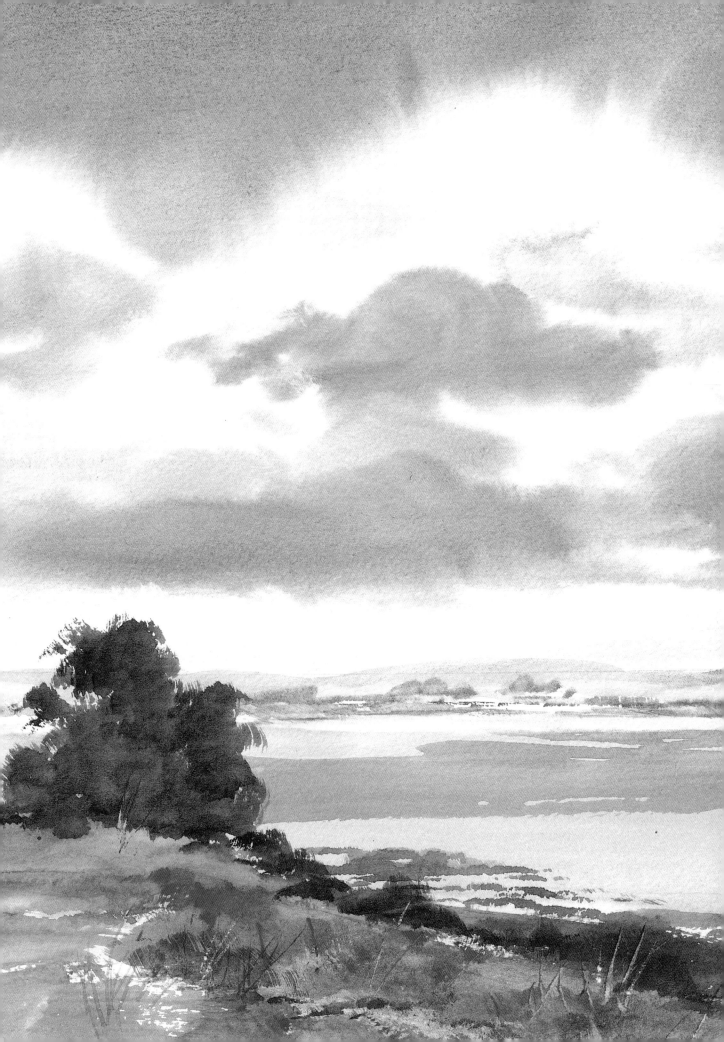

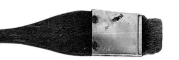

sky condition predominates. In other words, don't put in shadow if your sky is dull and overcast, but if you have a bright sky with cumulus clouds, their shadows should appear in the landscape. This may sound obvious, but I have often seen a painting of a yellow sky with a blue river underneath it.

STUDYING SKIES

Photographing skies will develop the observational skills you need in order to be able to paint them authentically. I am constantly surprised at the lack of knowledge of skies displayed by my students, even though they see them every day. Consulting a more specialized book on the subject will help you enormously, but here is a brief description of the most usual clouds to set you on your way.

Cirrus clouds are the high, wispy clouds that sometimes blow into long drifts, forming "mare's tails" or creating the light ripples known as "mackerel skies."

Cumulus clouds are my favorites. White and fluffy, flat-bottomed, and with a cauliflower-shaped top, they are exciting to paint but need practice as well as understanding if they are to be portrayed with authority.

Nimbus are the low, heavy, gray clouds that are often an indication of rain to come.

DESIGN

Let's look now at the actual painting of skies, thinking first about design. Although we've dealt with composition and design on pages 22–31, there are some principles that are particularly relevant to skies.

I have already mentioned balance and unity; another design rule is to provide contrast of value, which can be introduced by setting a dark tree against the lighted part of the sky, or

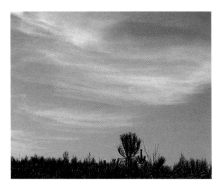

Here is a good example of cirrus clouds, which are commonly known as mare's tails. These can be used in an otherwise plain sky to create visual interest without detracting from the foreground subject.

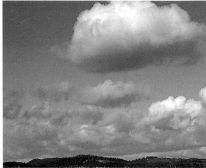

Cumulus clouds are an exciting addition to any landscape. Notice how perspective makes the clouds appear smaller as they recede into the distance. The blue of the sky is used to create a negative shape, forming the clouds.

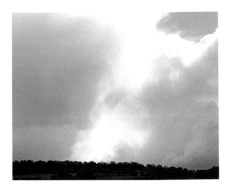

Cumulo-nimbus clouds form a majestic backdrop to a landscape. They create an ominous, dramatic atmosphere.

a sunlit spire against a thundercloud. Remember that variation is essential, so never have a row of identical clouds; one of them must always be dominant. A clear sky will need gradation—there is no such thing as a flat blue sky.

TECHNIQUE

The sky is an area of painting in which the hake brush is invaluable. It can sweep across the paper quickly, and its very size prevents overworking—the worst enemy of a good sky. To obtain this sweep, I push my chair back and stand up, giving myself plenty of room for a unified stroke, using my whole arm.

You cannot take a long time over a watercolor sky; if you do, you will end up with what I think of as a cardboard cutout effect. I invariably put a very weak raw sienna wash over the whole sky area and try to complete the entire sky while the wash is still damp.

Don't despair if your first efforts are weak and too runny. Usually the problem is too high a water content. Once you have learned to control the ratio of water to paint, things will improve dramatically. Remember that a sky always fades by about 30 percent when dry, so don't be timid about applying color. Remember, too, that any strong darks in the foreground painted later will also push the sky back.

Lack of confidence will probably show up more in skies than in any other area of your painting. The only way to gain confidence is to keep painting skies. After all, the sky will dictate the whole mood of a painting, so it's surely worth a little dedication to produce the best.

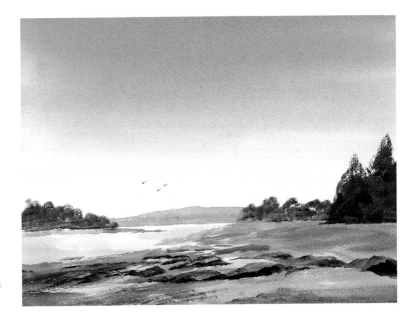

In a graded-wash sky the first step is a weak wash of raw sienna. Blue is then put in strongly at the top, with pressure taken off the brush as it moves back and forth to the horizon. If the paper is at an angle of 45 degrees, gravity will do the rest.

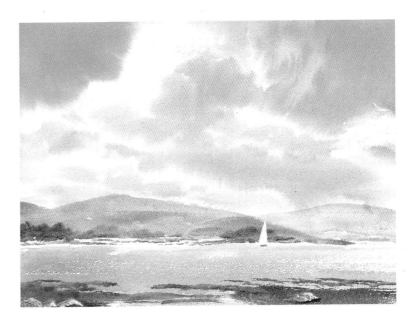

Here is a painted example of a typical cumulus sky similar to the one shown in the center photograph on the facing page. A sky of this type needs a simple foreground, as one that has plenty of interest in it will compete for the viewer's attention. A point to remember is that one cloud must always be dominant—but make sure you provide weight elsewhere in the painting or the end result will be unbalanced.

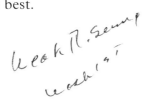

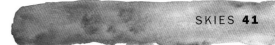

Evening Light, Severn Estuary

This demonstration shows how important it is to reflect sky colors in the foreground. In a subject with a rather flat expanse such as this, colors visible in a photograph may not provide lively enough interest in a painting, so you'll need to enhance them.

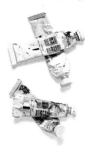

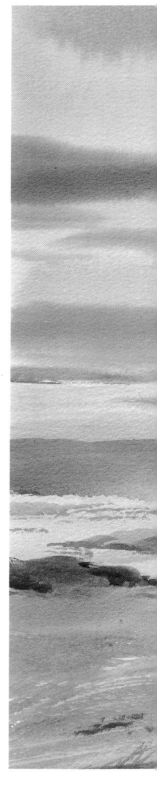

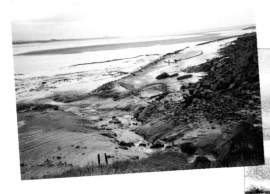

THE PHOTOGRAPH

This was a very exciting photograph to take. I shot it about a mile from my home, with the notorious Severn tide at its lowest. The camera's automatic exposure was influenced by the light of the sky, so inevitably, the foreground is too dark. Nevertheless, this is a good example of the fleeting effects that can be captured only with a camera, as the light would have changed long before I could have completed even the quickest of sketches in watercolor.

THE VALUE SKETCH

When I did my value sketch, I made a better lead into the picture by altering the angle and extent of the foreground stream. The viewer's eye is then taken through to the distant building, following the zigzag design of the sandbar.

THE PAINTING

When painting the scene, it was important to provide unity by reflecting all the existing sky colors in the wet mud and sand; it's easy to make this type of foreground very monotonous by using too few colors. The soft wet-into-wet clouds are a good foil to the crisp directional strokes of the foreground. A distant power station, although tiny, provides another point of interest.

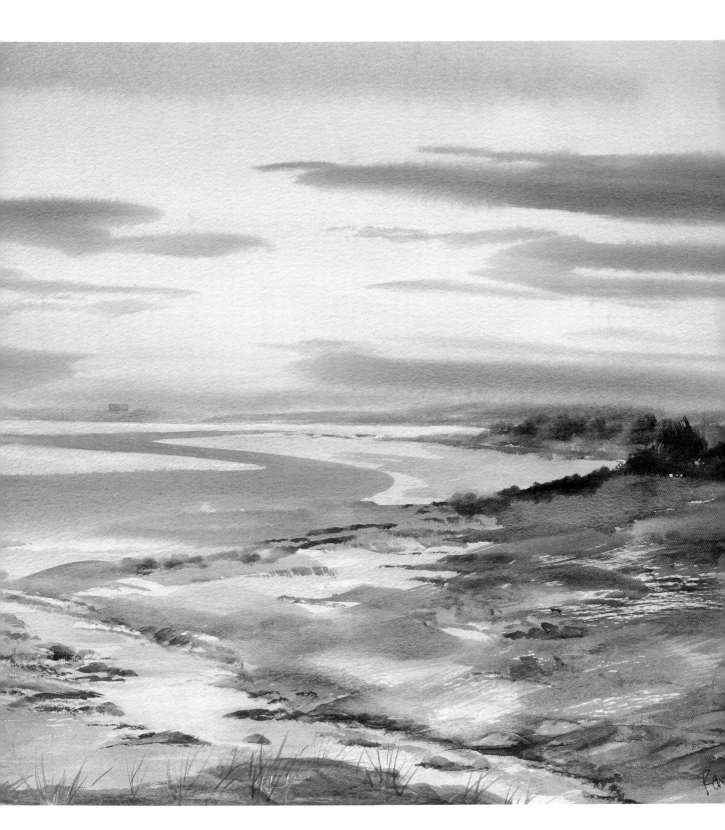

Evening Light, Severn Estuary, 14 x 18'' (35.5 x 45 cm)

Last of the Snow

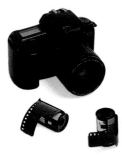

By borrowing a lowering sky from another photo, I give a suitably wintry effect to a landscape embellished with lingering patches of snow. Using your imagination in this way can produce art that is radically different from photographic references.

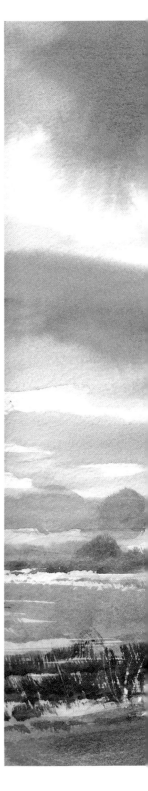

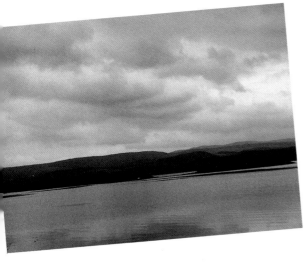

THE PHOTOGRAPHS

These two photographs, on loan to me by students from one of my classes, were combined in one painting. The photograph at left shows a cumulo-nimbus sky, which was reasonably straightforward to paint. The landscape in the photograph below left lacked balance, but masking off the pile of logs improved the scene considerably.

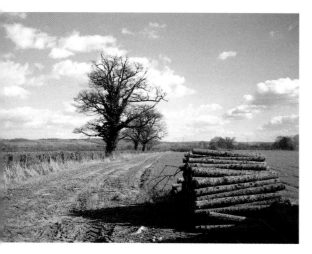

THE PAINTING

Only three colors were needed for this sky: the original raw sienna wash followed by a strong mixture of Payne's gray and alizarin crimson. For this type of sky you must steel yourself to put the color in much stronger than seems necessary. Your board should be on a slope so that the paint can diffuse downward naturally, without help from your brush. Notice how just one cloud dominates the sky, the rest being reduced as they reach the horizon. When I painted the landscape beneath, I changed the colors, exaggerated the rise of the land toward the horizon, and deliberately left areas of untouched paper to suggest snow. The winter trees are painted mainly with the rigger brush and finished off with dry brushstrokes of the hake.

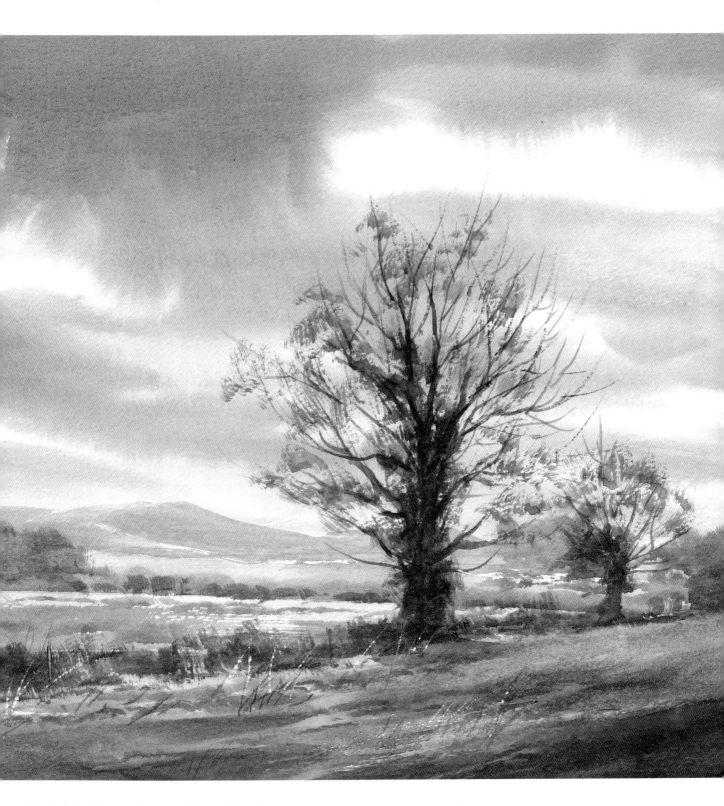

Last of the Snow, 12 x 14" (30 x 35.5 cm)

Evening on the Loch

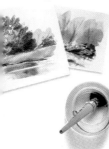

Here, two very different scenes were combined, using the restless sky in one photograph to contrast dramatically with the still calm of the loch in the other. This demonstration shows how it pays to be adventurous with your stock of sky photographs rather than limiting yourself to obvious matches.

THE PHOTOGRAPHS

The somewhat chaotic evening sky in the top photograph is full of color and excitement, but as so often happens, the landscape that lies beneath it is boring as well as being underexposed, and certainly not suitable for painting. The photograph below, however, shows a good lead into a pleasing scene, though the foreground needed cropping and the horizon lowering in order to allow more room for the sky in the painting. The photograph also contains some strong texture in the foreground, which I included in the painting to form a good textural contrast with the sky above.

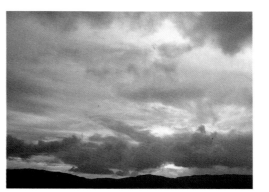

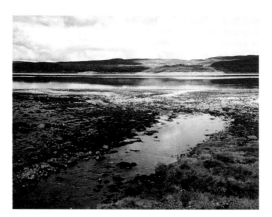

THE PAINTING

When you are painting a sky such as this, use the photograph simply as a reference—not that you would consider executing an exact copy, of course, but in this instance, it would really be quite impossible. The cloud was done in stages: first the raw sienna wash with added yellow was laid, then the main grays made from alizarin crimson and Payne's gray were dropped in while the background was still very damp. I changed the color of some of the clouds by adding raw sienna and a touch of burnt umber to warm them up, and made those near the horizon smaller. The landscape was taken from the second photograph, but of course, all the colors have been changed so that they match the sky. This repetition of sky color in the landscape is extremely important. Not only is it a good unifying device, but without it, the scene would be totally lacking in authenticity.

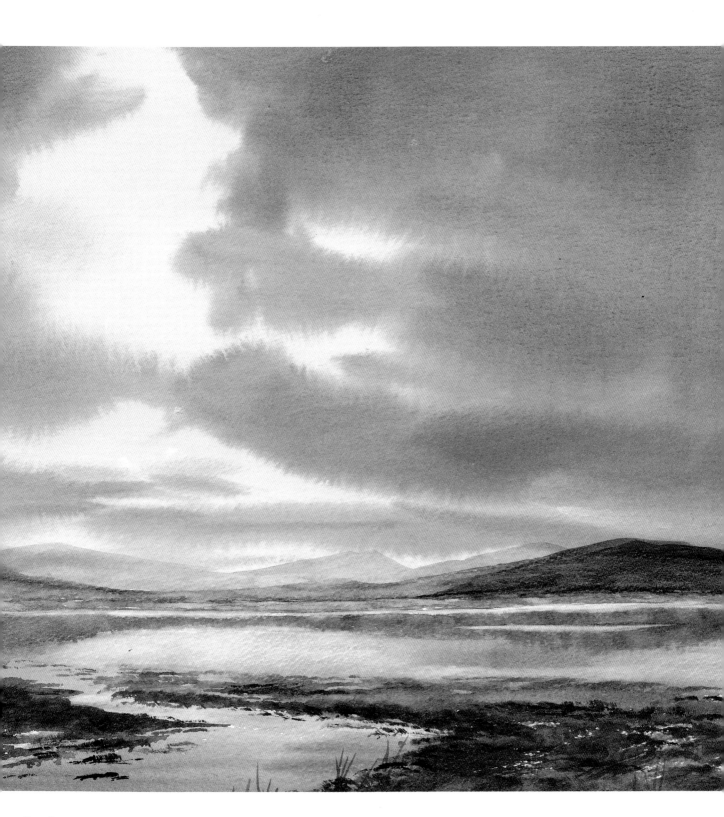

Evening on the Loch, 12 x 14" (30 x 35.5 cm)

Donegal Lakes

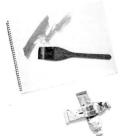

This demonstration shows that it's worth taking a further look for sky references, even when the one in your chosen landscape photo may seem acceptable. Though the picture on the right below has an attractive sky, my painting is greatly enhanced by borrowing a more dramatic cloud pattern from the photo on the left.

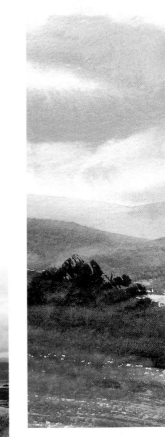

THE PHOTOGRAPHS

The picture on the left below shows masses of cumulus cloud, built up in layers. In order to obtain the right exposure for the sky, the landscape beneath had to be sacrificed. The photograph below right, of a typical scene in Donegal, Ireland, shows good recession, with cool colors for the mountain and warmer browns and ochres in the foreground.

THE PAINTING

I decided on a change of hue for this sky, so I used Prussian blue.

I painted it in patches, leaving the original raw sienna wash showing through in places to form the cream clouds. It is sometimes difficult to think of clouds in this way as negative shapes. I took care to paint the whole sky while the raw sienna wash was still damp in order to avoid "cardboard cutout" clouds. The gray shadows under the clouds were painted in Payne's Gray and alizarin crimson.

When painting the landscape I used Prussian blue in the mix to indicate the distance of the mountains, then gradually worked forward in stages, warming and strengthening my colors until I reached the foreground.

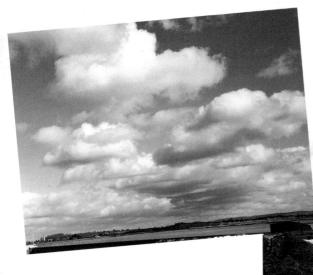

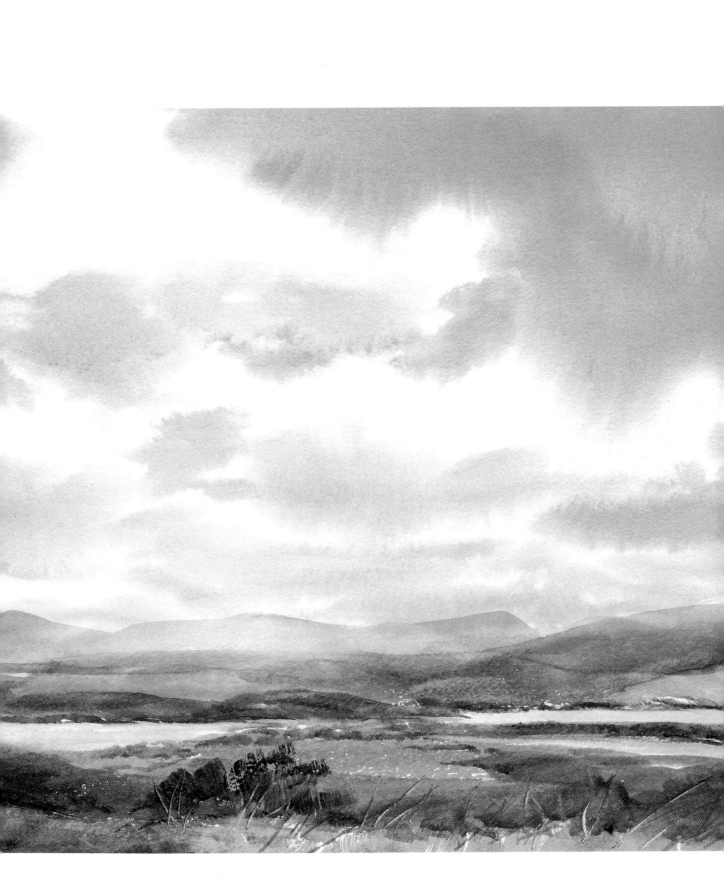

Donegal Lakes, **12 x 14"(30 x 35.5 cm)**

PROJECTS: Skies

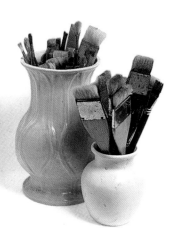

Here are several photographs of skies for you to use as the basis for paintings. They are intended merely to act as a guide—it's impossible when painting a free watercolor sky either from a photo or on location to reproduce it exactly. What you should attempt to do is to convey the essence of a skyscape. Look at the sky, think about how you are going to portray it, then let go, painting as quickly and boldly as possible. You will find it a really exhilarating experience. Study each of these photographs carefully and decide whether you need to make compositional changes to the landscapes. You will find my interpretations of them on pages 116–117.

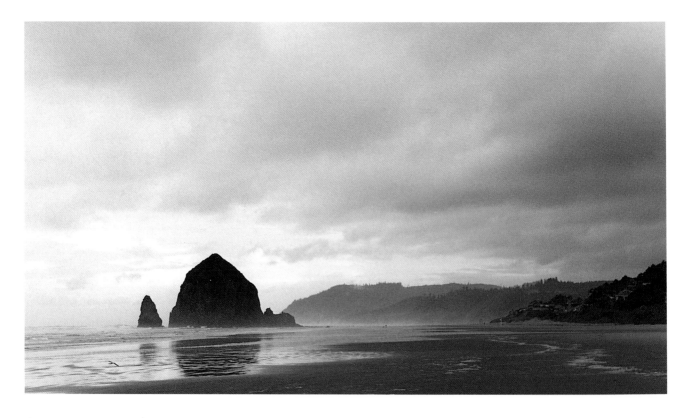

▲ *Haystack Rock in Oregon is a famous landmark on America's Pacific Coast and is, of course, the main object of interest in this photograph. To improve compositional balance, a painting will need the counterweight of a heavy cloud to the right of the scene. The beach in the foreground is a little featureless, so you should try to introduce some interesting texture and color here. The sea could be made rougher and spray used effectively to add movement to the scene. Seagulls, too, are a good source of movement and interest in a sea painting.*

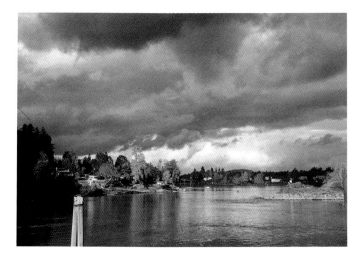

◄ This photograph, taken from a house in Oregon, is full of dramatic light and color and you should exploit these qualities as fully as possible in your painting. The foreground posts are a distraction and should be removed, but your painting will benefit from the addition of a more pleasing foreground object to add interest. The main focus here, though, is the boiling sky, so make the most of it.

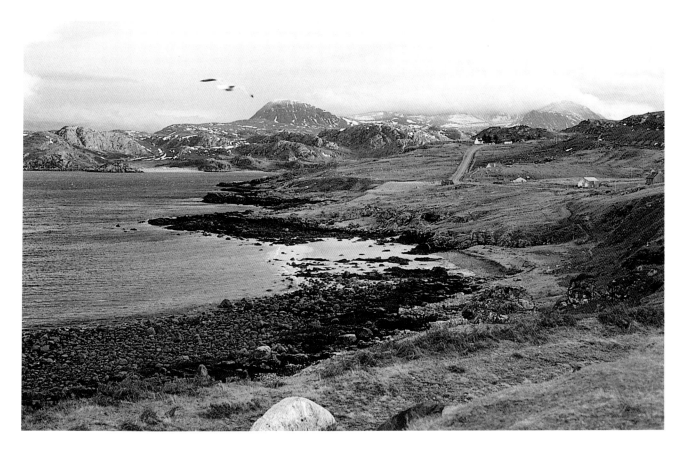

▲ Here, low cloud envelopes the top of the hills, but the impact of the sky is less than it might be because the horizon is high. I think the horizon needs to be dropped down the paper in order to allow more space for the sky, while still leaving sufficient room to provide texture and color in the landscape itself. Your object here is to create an interesting sky, but not one that will dominate the painting. You will also need to create a main object of interest. Any man-made object, even if it is very small, will stand out in a natural environment, so adding a fishing boat would be a solution—but you should think carefully about how to position it.

TREES AND WOODLAND

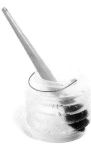

It is with this subject that the greatest difference between the photographic image and the final painting occurs. If you photograph a woodland scene, or even a single tree, the resultant image will show thousands of individual leaves, twigs, and branches. It would be impossible to paint each one, and in any case, you should not aspire to. Your aim is to produce a fresh impression, using all the atmosphere and depth of the scene without the detail.

SEEING THE STRUCTURE

Trees are beautiful in their own right and are an asset to any landscape painting, so they deserve careful study. As with any other subject, trees cannot be depicted well if you rely only on photographic references for knowledge of them. Take every opportunity to look carefully at trees in all seasons. For example, in winter, a deciduous tree will show you its skeleton, giving you a chance to learn the basic shape beneath the summer leaf canopy. Notice how distant trees lose their individuality and become a single overall mass.

Whether or not they appear in your photograph, it's important to leave "sky holes" in your painting in which to indicate branches and twigs. Never paint branches on top of foliage masses. Gradually thin branches as they reach the outside edges of a tree, combining them with the holes to form an interesting silhouette.

Just as important as the trees themselves is what grows beneath them. Foreground undergrowth should be contrasting and full of variation, but avoid the temptation to put in too much detail by painting quickly and lightly. Many a painting is spoiled by an overworked, muddy foreground.

CHOOSING COLORS

At every time of year you will have to use a far greater range of tree colors than those shown in your photographs in order to avoid a flat, monotonous effect. In a fall woodland scene, for example, I start painting with a variety of mauves in the background, giving an impression of distant fall foliage. This gradually changes to rich reds and browns in the foreground. In winter, a variety of blues and browns dominate; burnt umber and ultramarine used in varying proportions are what is most needed; a higher proportion of blue in the back, and more burnt umber at the front. Even a single tree should have a variety of colors in it.

Foreground trunks must never be a plain untextured brown. If you observe tree trunks carefully, you will discover a variety of grays, pinks, and even blues. Side lighting in your painting will help to emphasize the roundness of the trunk and to anchor the tree to the ground. It

Morning Sunshine
16 x 12"
(40.5 x 30 cm)
Here I painted the sky first and then dropped in the distant woodland wet-into-wet, keeping the colors very cool. Working forward, I added progressively more warmth and also strengthened the bare trees. The branches were put in with the rigger. The water went in as a very pale raw sienna wash, and I immediately dropped in the reflections wet-into-wet. Those of the main trunks were put in with rich paint so they would register strongly. Finally, I used white gouache to paint strong light edging the tree trunks.

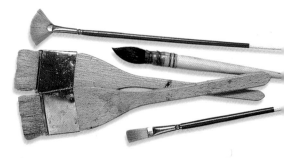

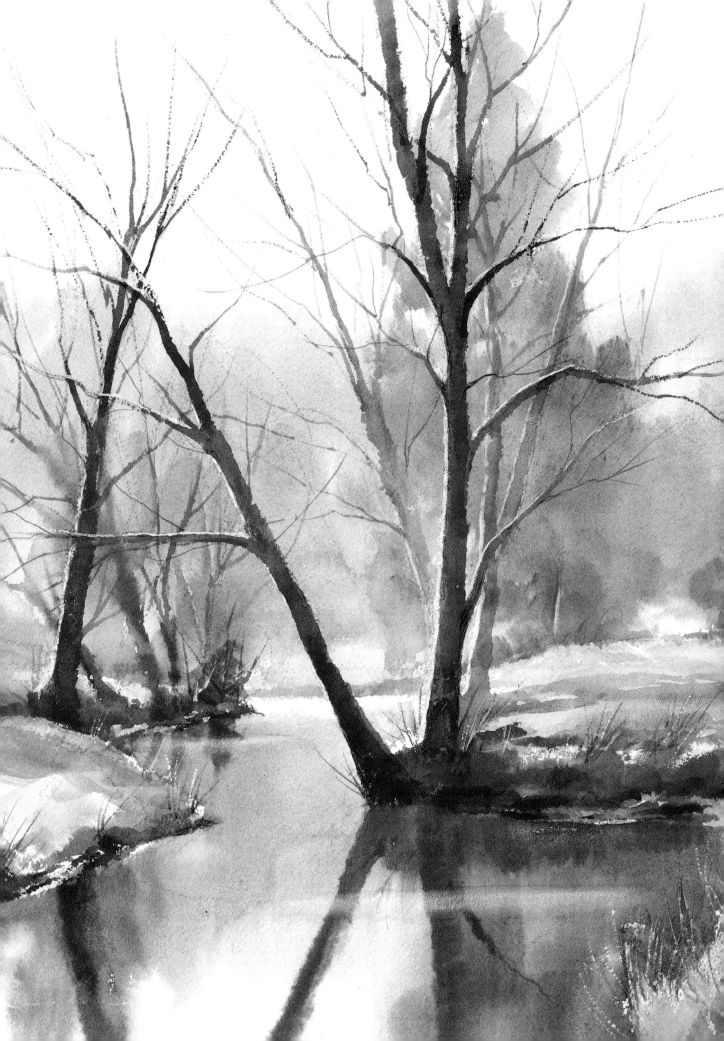

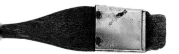

also offers an opportunity to create contrast and excitement with interesting shadows, whether they are present in your reference photograph or not. If you want to portray a very large tree, show only a small part of it in order to suggest its massive bulk.

USING THE RIGHT BRUSHES

The only two brushes I use for trees are the hake and the rigger. For distant trees, I employ the corner of the hake to produce the ragged profile of trees against the horizon, then a gentle touch with the edge to create the base of the wood.

I use a sideways motion with the edge of the hake to represent the trunks more to the fore. I then switch to the rigger to delineate branches and twigs, using varying pressure—heavy for the thicker branches where they come off the trunk, and reducing to a feather-light touch for the finest twigs. It takes practice with the rigger to produce authentic tapering branches, but it is time well spent, especially when you are

painting winter trees. Tapping the paper with the back of the hake produces very realistic foreground foliage that does not look overworked. The rigger is the brush to use for grasses and undergrowth beneath the trees, but do be economical with it, just suggesting grasses rather than overworking them.

DEPTH OF FIELD

In a photograph, a foreground tree has virtually the same value as a distant one, whereas in a painting, you will need to create depth of field by deliberately cooling color in the distance and massing the trees together as one single unit. As you move forward in the painting, warm the color, reserving the richest tones and detail for the foreground. In other words, exaggerate the aerial perspective. You need to bear in mind that you are trying to portray on a flat piece of paper a scene that may stretch back miles from the viewer. While a distant hillside may consist of thousands of trees, it can

◄ *This shows how the rigger is used to depict fine branches on winter trees. The width of the branch is dictated by the amount of pressure on the brush, which is held at the top end to allow freedom. You may need a fair amount of practice before you can produce these winter trees with confidence and conviction, but it will be time well spent.*

Rigger

◄ *The basic method for painting summer trees is to tap the back of the hake on the paper to produce the foliage, leaving plenty of gaps. The branches are then put in with the rigger—but only in the empty spaces. Never paint in branches on top of the foliage.*

be convincingly expressed by just the swift stroke of the hake brush.

I very much enjoy painting misty woodland, as I love the wet-into-wet effects I can achieve at the back of the scene. The whole of the background is painted wet-into-wet, even the rigger work, which, of course, diffuses. As the paper dries, I move forward so that the trees become sharper and warmer as they reach the foreground.

When you are painting woodland, your aim should be to give the viewer the feeling of being able to walk into the woods. Woodland scenes often incorporate pathways, and these should wander rather than being straight. Use an exaggerated perspective so that paths take the eye right into the scene. This is one of the many changes you may have to make to your original photograph. One of the most frequent faults in photographs of woodland is that they do not have enough depth of field, so you will need to rectify this in your painting.

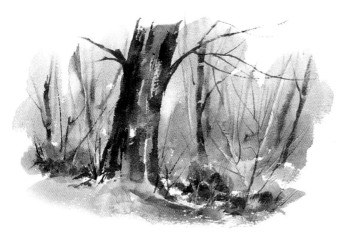

▲ *This illustration shows a woodland scene and demonstrates the texture of a foreground trunk. The background has been kept deliberately wet-into-wet in order to avoid a conflict of interest. The foreground undergrowth is painted in much richer, stronger paint. The main trunk has been painted with the hake; everything else has been put in by using the rigger and a fingernail.*

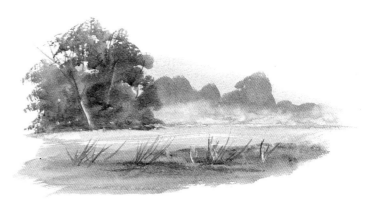

▲ *Using cool and warm colors as shown here creates depth in a landscape. I have added more water to the paint at the base of the distant trees to give an impression of mist. Don't overdo foreground texture; often, just a hint is sufficient.*

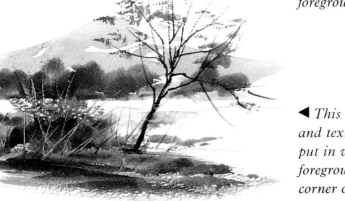

◀ *This is a good example of foreground grasses and texture. Again, the background trees have been put in wet-into-wet to push them back, while the foreground is put in with richer paint. I've used the corner of a credit card to create the light grasses, scratching them out while the paint is still damp.*

Misty Creek

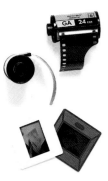

The comparison between the photograph and the finished painting here is an excellent demonstration of what this whole book is about. The painting is a distillation of the photograph rather than a reproduction of it, improving upon the composition and enhancing the mysterious atmosphere of the location.

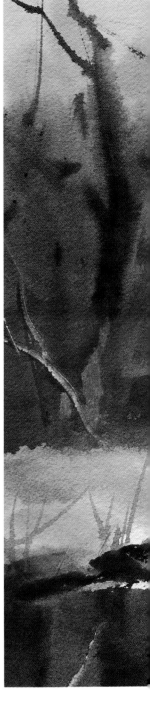

THE PHOTOGRAPH

This photograph of a creek, lent to me by my friend Dr. Don Fisher, is highly evocative of the raw feel of a damp and misty day in winter. However, it was taken in the poor light conditions that inevitably prevail at such times and is therefore lacking in definition and contrast, so the scene appears dull and rather flat. However, it offered me an opportunity to use my imagination to produce a moody and exciting watercolor by adding more contrast in hue and value. I also needed to simplify the whole scene by clearing away all unnecessary clutter, starting with the tufts of vegetation that are just visible at the very bottom of the photograph.

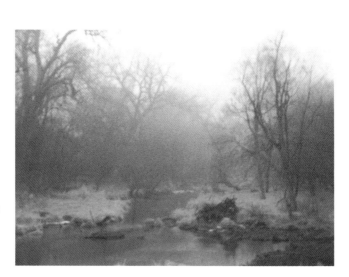

THE PAINTING

This is essentially a wet-into-wet painting. First I covered the whole paper with a raw sienna wash and then I dropped in the trees and foliage with various strengths of paint, sometimes applying pigment almost undiluted. I had to work very quickly and freely, using my fingernail to delineate the light branches, and a piece of credit card to scrape off the tops of the rocks. The sparkle on the water was obtained with a very fast and light stroke of the hake.

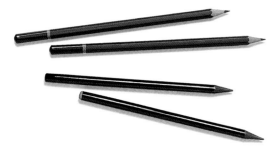

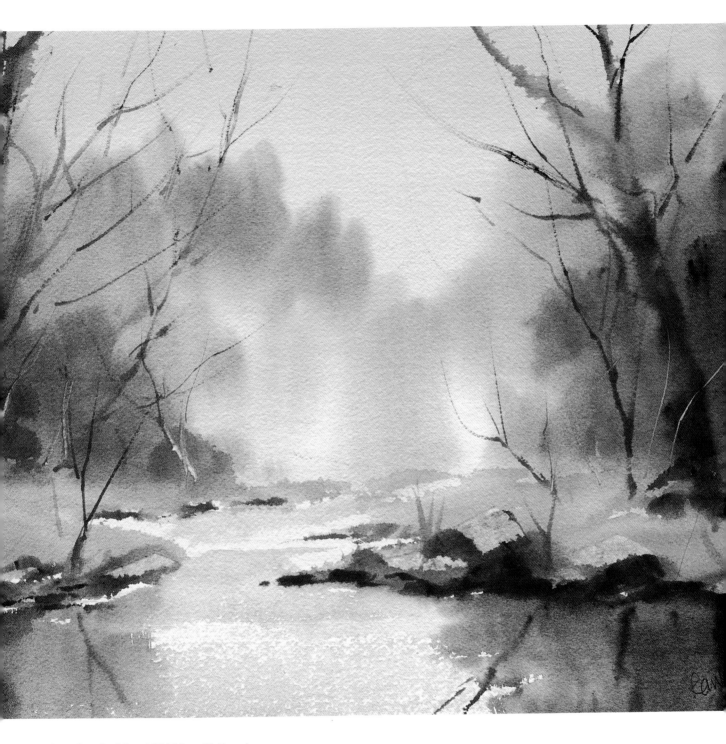

Misty Creek, 12 x 16" (30 x 40.5 cm)

Winter Shadows

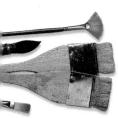

The photograph and painting here demonstrate how even a small alteration of color or shape can have a major impact on the design of a picture, turning a rather unbalanced photograph into a painting that is compositionally satisfying.

THE PHOTOGRAPH

I derived much enjoyment both from taking this photograph of a wintry field and converting it into a watercolor. However, the photograph lacks balance, with nothing to counterweight the strong shape of the trees to the left. The right side has no point of interest to contain the viewer's eye within the scene.

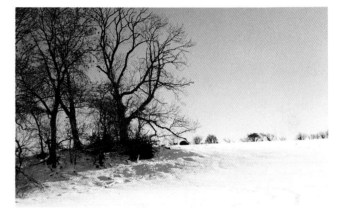

THE PAINTING

When I painted the scene, I corrected the composition simply by lengthening the shadows so that they stretched all the way across the field to the right-hand side of the picture. I also made a little more of the far trees on that side of the picture. The tree skeletons cried out for plenty of calligraphy via the rigger, which contrasted well with the indistinct mass of the distant trees. When I was painting in the shadows, I had to work with speed and decisiveness as there was no second chance there; shadows must be kept transparent. The untouched snow was left as completely white paper.

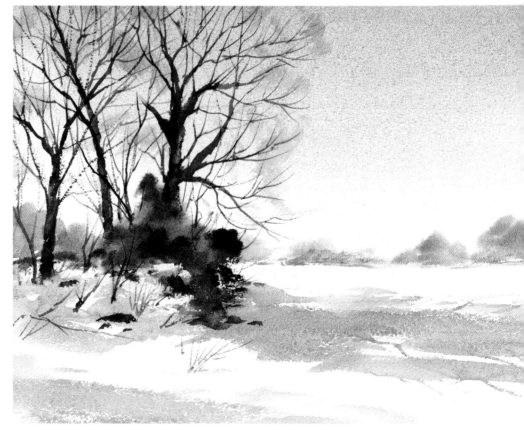

Winter Shadows, 11 x 14" (28 x 35.5 cm)

River Bend

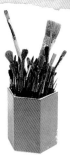

Trees cast strong reflections in water, which always adds abundant interest to a painting. The light on the water here has been exaggerated, heightening reflections even more.

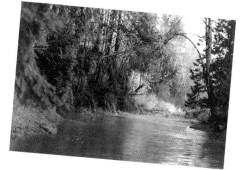

THE PHOTOGRAPH

What drew me to this scene was the contrasting pinks and greens of the vegetation complemented by mauve reflections cast by the trees.

THE PAINTING

After painting the sky, I worked all the background woodland wet-into-wet, using alizarin crimson and ultramarine. Once it was dry, I painted the foreground woods with rich green, dropping in plenty of reds at the base to break the monotony of a single hue. Pinks and mauves of distant trees were repeated in the riverbank shadows, providing unity. Tree trunks were added via sideways strokes of the hake. Finally, I painted the river itself, using vertical, wet-into-wet brushstrokes to describe tree reflections. A sunlit patch of water provides the painting with a bright center of interest.

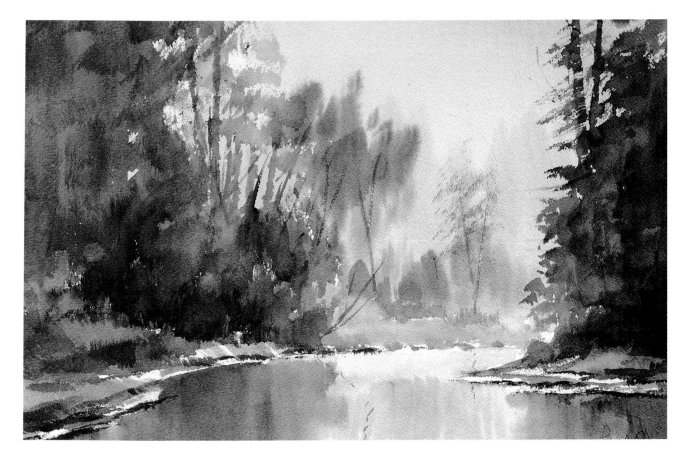

River Bend, 12 x 16" (30 x 40.5 cm)

The White Barn

Some photographs are suitable only as a reference point for certain aspects of a painting; others stand quite well as pictures in their own right, needing just minimal alteration to make a satisfying watercolor.

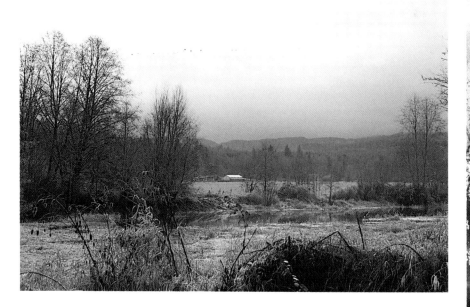

THE PHOTOGRAPH

This picture is pleasing in both composition and color, so very little design change was needed to transform it into watercolor. However, as the white barn is the main object of interest, I decided to make minor alterations to focus the viewer's attention firmly upon it.

THE PAINTING

I decided that some minor trees in the middle distance would be best eliminated so that they would not distract the eye from the barn. I also left out some tree branches on the right to achieve a less cluttered look, and cleared away a bit of foreground brush to allow easier access into the picture. The main difference between the photograph and painting, though, is that to provide more warmth and contrast, I made the distant colors richer, introducing purples mixed from alizarin crimson and ultramarine. These contrasted well with the warm colors of the field and riverbank. I used purple again in the foreground, creating more unity in the painting. I also moved the area of heaviest cloud, lifting it from the horizon to allow greater delineation between hills and sky.

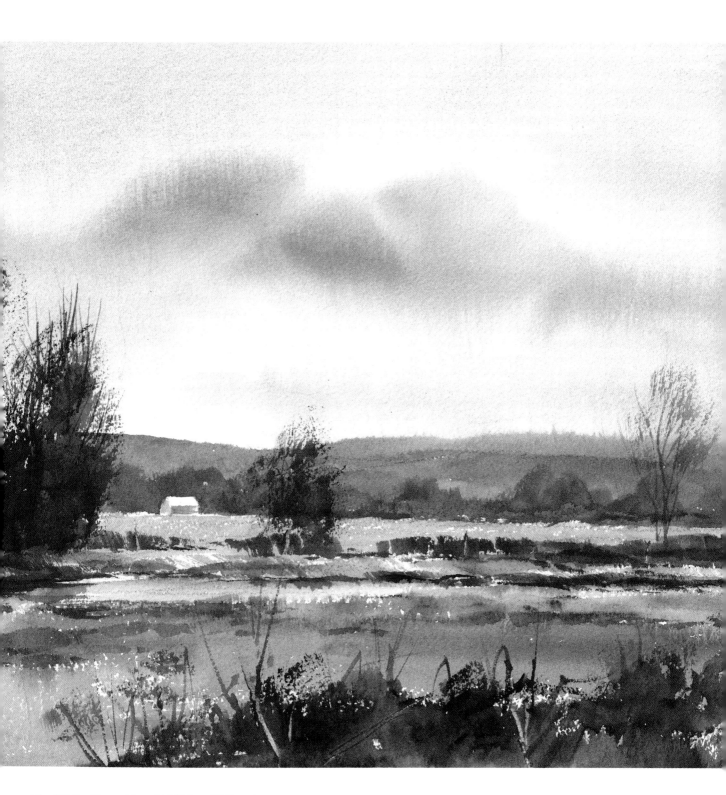

The White Barn, 12 x 16" (30 x 40.5 cm)

Winter Reflections

This painting of the reflections of skeletal winter trees in water shows that it may be possible to use a photograph almost as is, without having to think about how to improve the composition or colors.

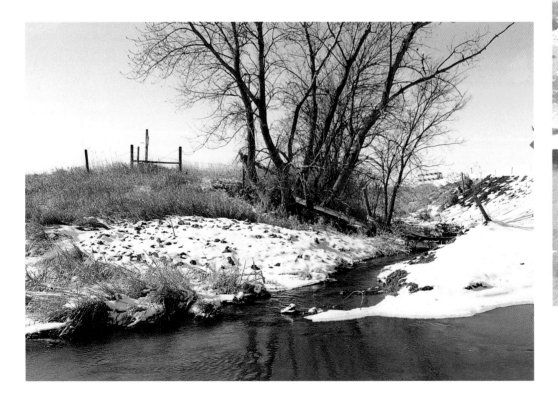

THE PHOTOGRAPH

Sometimes you may be fortunate enough to find a photograph that is full of potential and cries out to be painted as soon as possible. This is such a picture—an absolute natural. It needed almost no alteration.

THE PAINTING

Painting the graded-wash sky was a straightforward task. I laid in a thin raw sienna wash, then immediately applied a mixture of Prussian blue and ultramarine. Next, I put in the background scrub, which was a mix of raw sienna and light red, with the darker patches in ultramarine and light red. The group of trees was a delight to paint, using a rigger and dry-brush hake. The snow was mainly left as untouched paper. Now came the river, which had to be done quickly and decisively. A first wet wash of varied blue and raw sienna was followed immediately, wet-into-wet, with rich browns and blues for reflections. Finally, a few squiggles with undiluted paint indicated the tree trunks.

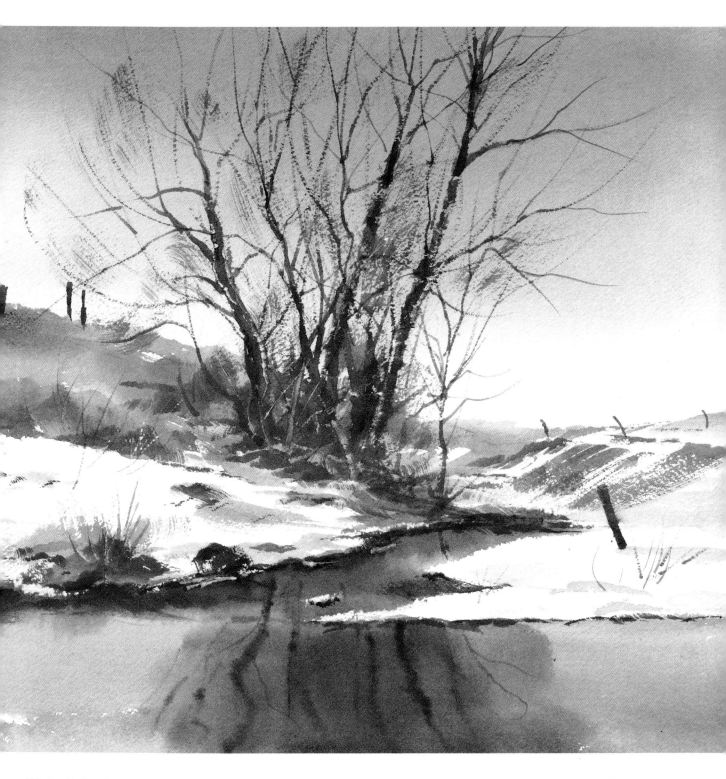

Winter Reflections, 12 x 16" (30 x 40.5 cm)

PROJECTS: Trees and Woodland

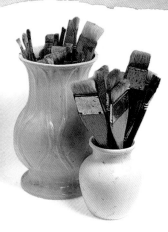

When you tackle these subjects, remember that although photographs may show every twig and leaf, your job is to produce your interpretation of trees and foliage. In other words, make a great effort to restrain yourself from close copying. Symbolize the scenes instead. Study each photo carefully and decide what changes you want to make. For example, you may wish to improve the composition or to eliminate certain aspects altogether. My interpretations of these photographs are on pages 118–19.

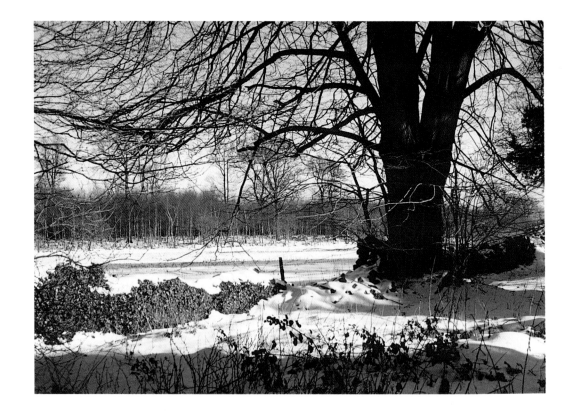

▲ *The main object of interest here is the tree, of course, plus the wonderful shadow patterns created by sun on snow. However, the strong shadow running across the bottom of the photograph seems to create a barrier, keeping the viewer out of the scene, so you may want to consider removing some or all of this in your painting. Think how you might draw the viewer's eye into the painting instead. The branches of the main tree will need to be simplified, and the distant woodland might also need some attention to make it more interesting.*

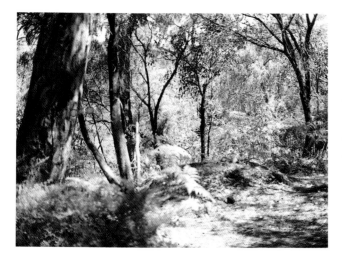

◄ *This photograph was taken on a very hot summer's day in the woods. Your main problem will be to create depth in your picture. You might decide to do this by keeping the greens in the distance fairly cool and painting them wet-into-wet, and then using warmer and stronger greens in the foreground. You will also need to simplify the picture considerably. Don't attempt to indicate every branch and leaf, even in the foreground. The temptation with this type of picture is to overwork, but you have to learn to stop as soon as you have captured the atmosphere. Try to retain the strong contrasts of light and shade in your painting.*

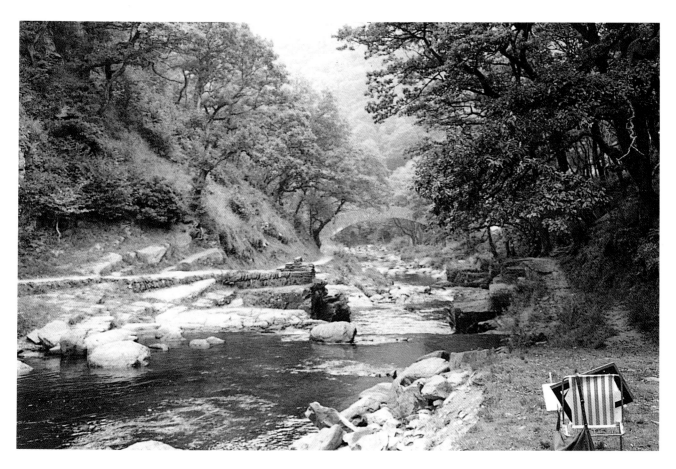

▲ *This type of scene lends itself ideally to watercolor. The composition of this photograph is fairly good, with important elements standing apart from the striped deckchair, which you will probably decide to remove. Again, you will need to* *think about creating depth, and how you will set about portraying the distant tree-covered hillside. You might consider moving some of the trees in order to allow a better view of the bridge and the hill in the background.*

WATER

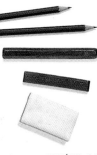

While skies are my favorite subject, water comes a close second. Looking at scores of my paintings in a recent exhibition, I realized that a very high percentage of them depicted water in one form or another. Of course, water appears in a wide range of subjects: boats, harbors, seashores, rivers, lakes, estuaries, waterfalls, even the humble puddle in the road. The mood can range from raging torrents to tranquil lakes.

TECHNIQUES FOR PAINTING WATER

When working from photographs, you will often have to make changes to the water in some way to make it look authentic in a painting. This can be done by using various techniques. For example, the tumbling white water of a fast-flowing river can be made to look really exciting by using fast strokes that follow the direction of the water, leaving plenty of white paper showing. Portraying still water, you may have to put in reflections that aren't in the photograph, perhaps because the surface was ruffled at the time. Reflections are an excellent way of unifying a painting. Conversely, I often wipe out a streak to indicate a patch of disturbed water, which adds interest. This is particularly effective where the water is darkest.

In the painting of water, the watchword is economy. Many water scenes are ruined by overworking. Hundreds of carefully painted ripples can kill a painting. Aim to put in a minimum of strokes, leaving some work to the viewer's imagination. The reflection of a post or tree in the water can be portrayed by just a slight wriggle of your brush, while untouched paper for white water can be just as descriptive as paint—but don't leave too many conflicting whites in other parts of the painting as they will dilute the effect.

When I paint a large stretch of open water, I often grade the wash from dark at the front to light toward the back to give the impression of depth, whether or not it appears in the photograph. The best way to do this is to paint the rest of the picture first then turn it upside down, put it on a sloping board and wet the whole surface of the water lightly. Put in a strong wash at the front, lessening the pressure on the brush as it moves toward the horizon, then allow gravity to do the rest. In that way, the line of the horizon will not be encroached upon.

PAINTING ROCKS

Another aspect of painting water scenes is the portrayal of rocks. Don't feel you must reproduce those in the photograph; you are quite free to take them out, reduce some, and enlarge others. They can supply contrast with the water— another feature of good design. Increase the contrast between the top and sides of the rocks to add drama to your composition.

Welsh River in Flood (detail)
This painting, based on a black-and-white photograph in a guide book, shows how leaving plain white paper conveys the feeling of rushing water. I have given depth to the scene by using restrained color in the background and strong, contrasting colors for the foreground rocks.

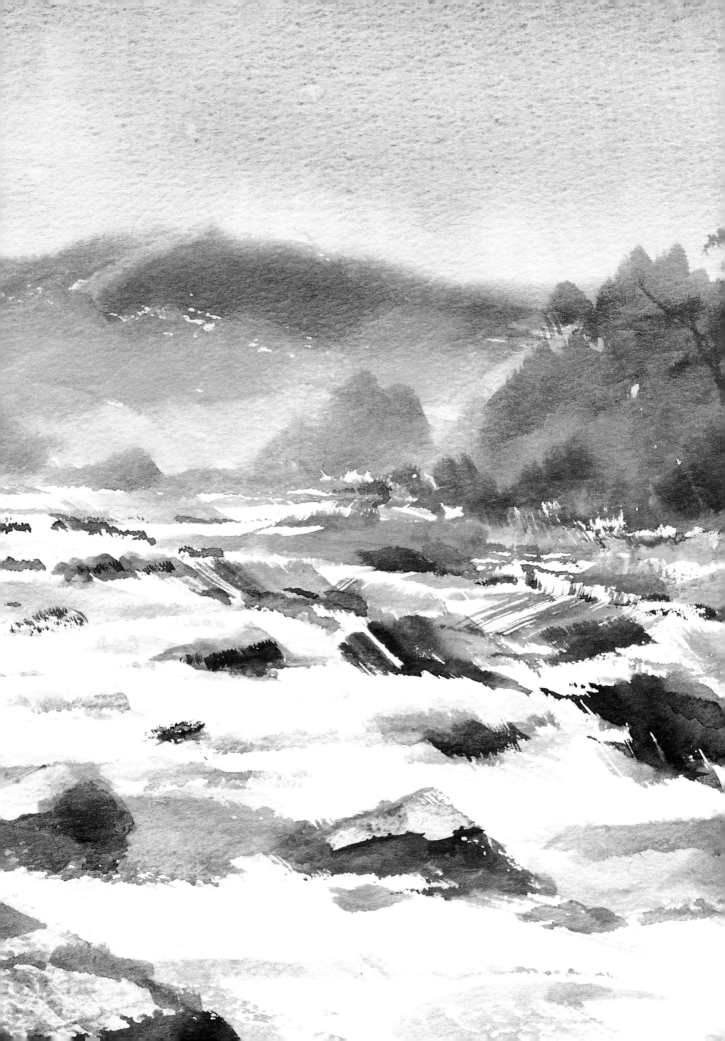

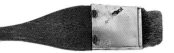

BRUSHSTROKES

Generally, I use the hake for my water scenes, employing it in many different ways. I love the sparkle it gives when it is used to make one sweep lightly and quickly across the sea or a lake. It just touches the surface of the paper, taking only seconds to do but giving an effect you could not obtain with hours of work. I particularly enjoy painting estuaries at low tide, where there are dry sandbanks which, again, have to be put in with one quick flourish of the brush to give them spontaneity, the wet sand and mud reflecting the colors of the sky.

When painting seascapes, I like to stand up and use my whole arm to produce spontaneous curves to depict the waves, leaving white paper for their crests. The shoreline, too, must be put in with simple sweeps and then left alone. Fiddling about with it afterward is always disastrous. Again, the hake brush is ideal for this type of work.

Water scenes very often include boats, and your main aim here should be to simplify them. You may be tempted to copy every detail you can see in the photograph, but as long as the overall proportions are right, it's surprising how little detail you actually need. The 1" (25 mm) flat, used judiciously and delicately, will do the job and prevent you from the overelaboration that might result from using a smaller brush. It is obviously important that the style of boats should match the context of the waterscape.

COLOR IN WATER PAINTINGS

Don't make the mistake of mixing up a wash of blue and painting the whole water surface, no matter how

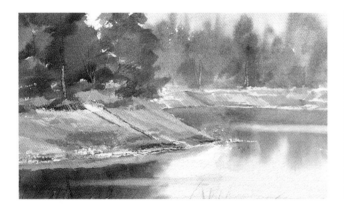

To paint these reflections in calm water, first I applied a thin wash of sky color and then brushed in the vague tree shapes vertically while the wash was still damp. I then used stronger, richer paint for the foreground reflections. The soft streaks were taken out with a dry hake while the paper was still damp.

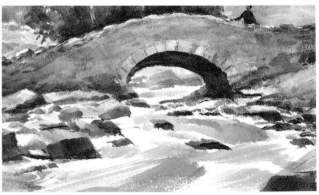

This fast-flowing river is portrayed by making full use of the white paper. The color has been put on with a hake, using fast, light strokes in the direction of the flow. Remember that the more economical the strokes are, the better the result will be.

large, with that one color. The surface of the ocean or a lake changes color constantly, especially in the shallows where sand or pebbles show through. This gradation of color, one of the fundamental principles of design, is particularly important here in order to avoid monotony.

Water itself is colorless but it reflects every hue around it, be it from the sky, from trees, or from buildings. However, sky color must always reflect in water and this interplay is critical in unifying a picture. It's important to remember this if you are using two separate photographs, one for sky and one for water.

Be careful not to be too influenced by the color of the water in a photograph. Many rivers will appear brown and muddy after rain, and such coloration will not make for an attractive painting. The color of the river should rely more on the sky above and trees around it rather than the mud particles within it, which also cut down reflections.

When depicting ponds or lakes, I paint in the general sky color first, then drop in the

reflections of whatever lies behind them in rich paint to compensate for the dampness of the surface. The blend will soften to produce a right effect, but will still appear in virtually the same tones as the original object.

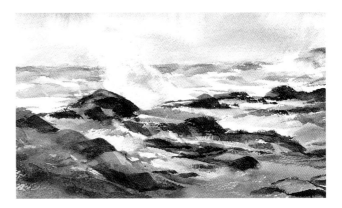

When depicting waves and rocks, the challenge is to convey the idea of opposition—fluid water moving against rigid rocks. The direction of brushstrokes and the use of white paper showing through will help produce this effect and create visual excitement. You should also drop in plenty of varied color.

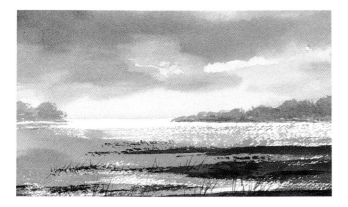

In this tranquil scene the water sparkles with reflected light. For this effect, first put in the sky, then take a hake brush full of the same color and sweep it very lightly and quickly across the water area so that it just catches the surface of the paper. When this is dry, you can put in the foreground shoreline.

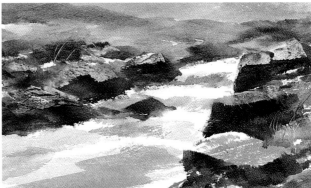

The main things to remember when painting rocks is that the tops must be light and the sides dark, and the color must be varied. In some of the rocks here, I used a piece of credit card while the paint was still wet to scrape off the top surfaces. In others, I painted the top surface light and used stronger, darker paint for the sides.

Oregon Lake

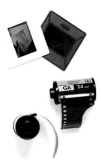

This demonstration shows how useful a value sketch can be when working from a photograph, particularly one with a variety of forms within it. A value sketch reduces the scene to a simple pattern of lights and darks and suggests how the tones of the photograph may be modified to increase depth and contrast.

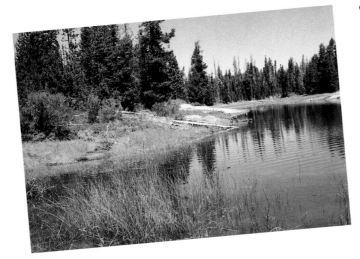

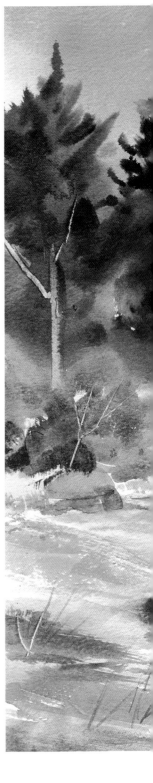

THE PHOTOGRAPH

I took this photograph while I was on family camp in the wilds of Oregon. There was plenty of interest here for a painting of water, with reflections of the sky and pine trees, rushes growing in the foreground, and a rippling of the water surface caused by a light breeze.

THE VALUE SKETCH

I wanted more depth and contrast in my painting of this lovely place, so I included some distant snow-covered mountains in my value sketch to guide that result. I also decided to add the family canoe drawn up on the bank to provide the scene with a necessary focus of interest. I altered the curve of the shoreline to draw the viewer's eye into the picture, and I also reduced the amount of rushes.

THE PAINTING

For my painting, I cooled the colors of the distant trees to create a feeling of recession, then strengthened the hues of the nearer trees on the left. Notice that the reflections in the water also follow these changes. They were put in wet-into-wet on top of the sky-colored water of the lake.

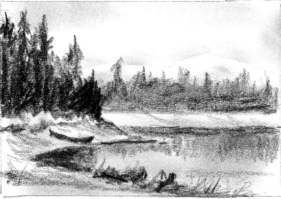

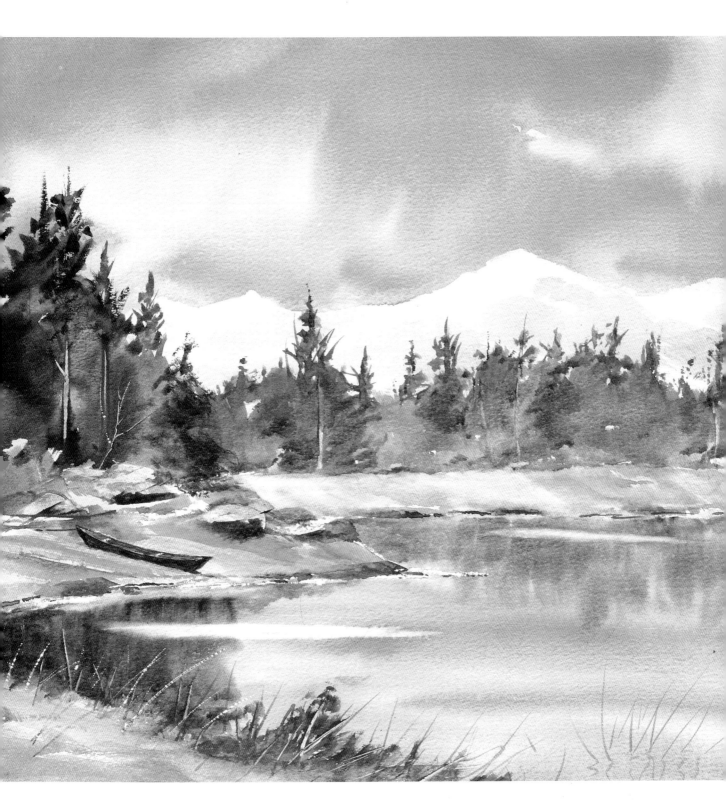

Oregon Lake, **13 x 17"** (33 x 43 cm)

Australian Peninsula

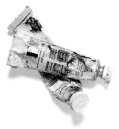

Often you may have to emphasize the lights and darks in a value sketch to obtain sufficient contrast in your finished painting. In a subject such as this, however, which contains dark landscape features and foaming white waves, you need do little to improve upon the scene.

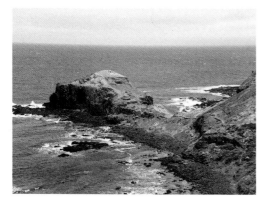

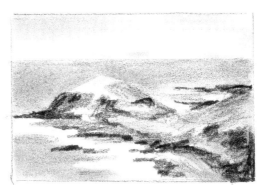

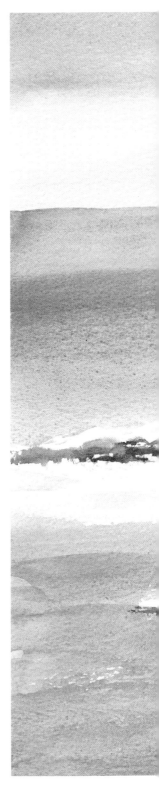

THE PHOTOGRAPH

I was attracted by this curiously shaped peninsula in Australia, with its starkly different planes and variety of textures ranging from the rocky beach to the smooth, well-worn path. With no distracting objects to mar the view, it was obvious that it would translate well into a painting.

THE VALUE SKETCH

My photograph contains plenty of contrasting light and dark in the white waves and dark rocks, so I did not have to search for more. The only significant change I made was to put a line of distant hills on the horizon, which existed in reality but did not show up in the photograph.

THE PAINTING

In the finished picture I have simplified the sea, for attempting to reproduce the waves too closely would only have resulted in a static effect. I have also introduced more color in the cliffs and beach by adding complementary mauves. Notice how the brushstrokes follow the general profile of the land mass to emphasize its form.

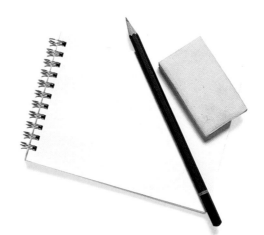

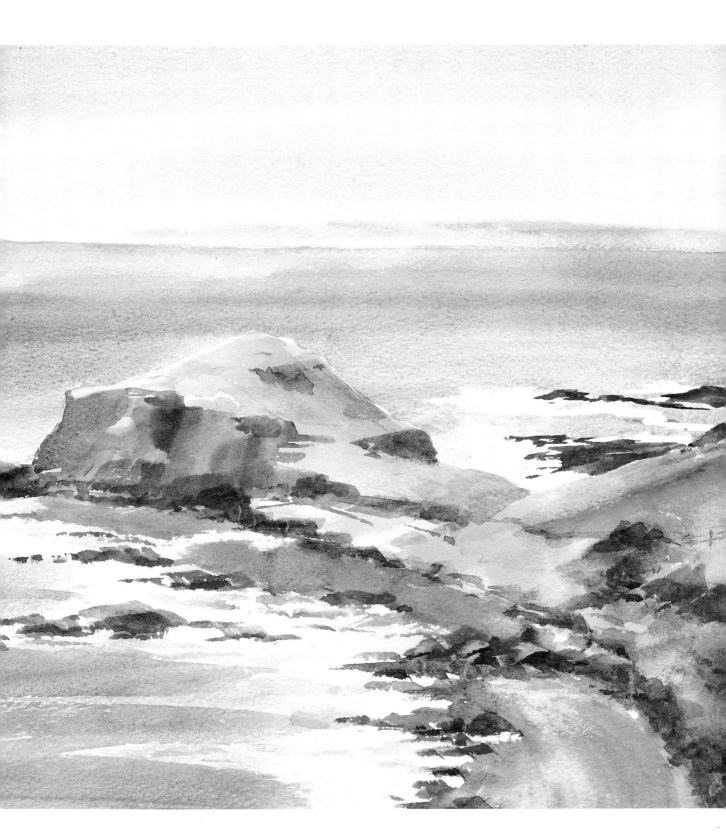

Australian Peninsula, 11 x 14'' (28 x 35.5 cm)

River Gorge

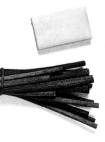

This example shows how a horizontal, landscape-shaped photograph can be changed to make a vertical, portrait-shaped painting. Altering the proportions of a scene in this way not only affects its composition but can also shift its emphasis considerably.

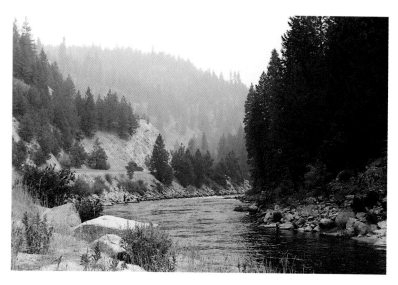

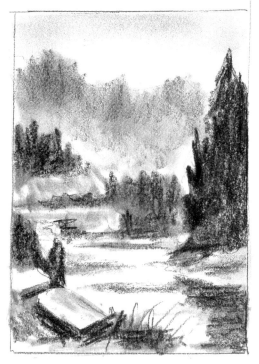

THE PHOTOGRAPH

It's always a help in altering proportions to use two or three pieces of white paper to crop the photograph in various ways, moving them around until you frame the most interesting section of the scene. In the above photograph, steep wooded banks along the river largely dominate the scene, but I wanted to focus the viewer's attention on the water.

THE VALUE SKETCH

By cropping the riverbanks, I have thrust the water into prominence so that it is now the main focus of attention. The sky also appears a more major part of the composition, though, in fact, its proportion in relation to the trees has not changed.

THE PAINTING

Note that I have made the water faster-flowing by leaving white paper to create the impression of foam, and have intensified much of the color in order to provide contrast and depth. Pinks have been repeated throughout the painting, giving a feeling of unity between the foreground, middle distance, and far distance.

River Gorge, **16 x 12" (40.5 x 30 cm)**

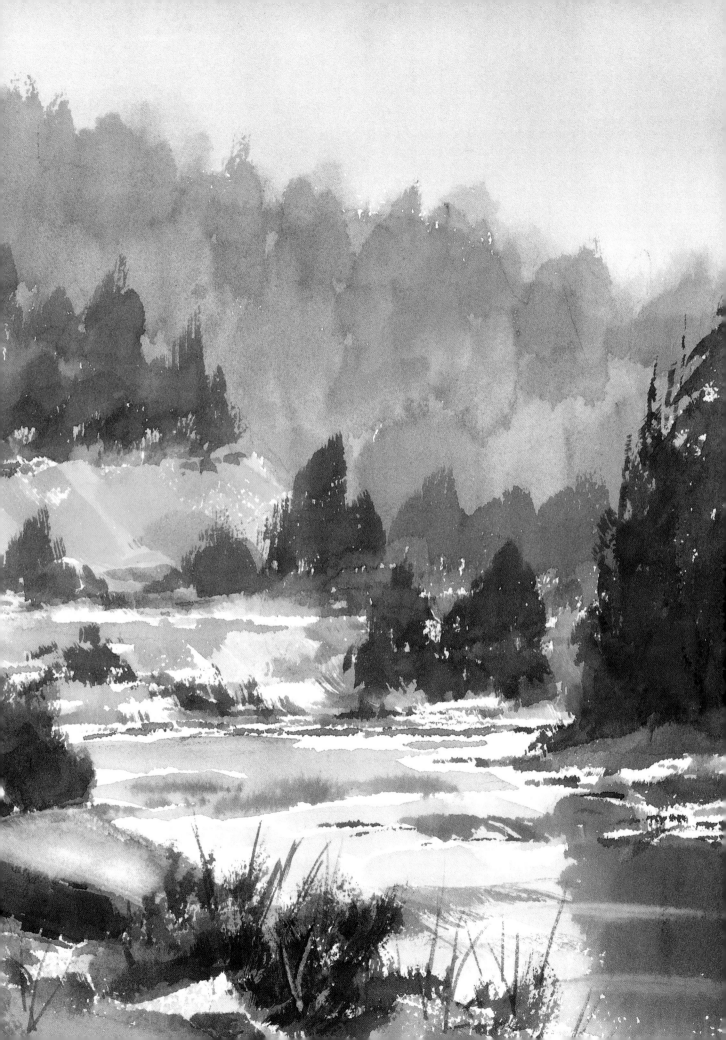

Misty Hills

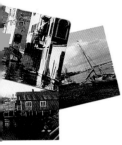

Sometimes a photograph dictates exactly how you should translate it into paint. The treatment to use here is unmistakably large areas of wet-into-wet to suggest watery and misty effects, with dry brush to point up foreground details.

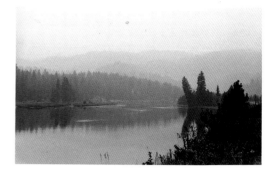

THE PHOTOGRAPH

The striking shape of this pair of trees caught my attention and I liked the way they were both reflected in the water and silhouetted against the misty hills behind them. All in all, it seemed an ideal photograph for an atmospheric painting in which the wet-into-wet technique would predominate.

THE PAINTING

It wasn't necessary to make many changes to this photograph other than straightening the leaning tree and leaving an area of mist behind both trees to produce a stronger focal point. Painting the river using a very wet-into-wet technique was all I needed to do to convey a realistic impression. I used dry brush technique on the foreground bank to provide contrast with the treatment of the river.

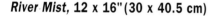

River Mist, **12 x 16"(30 x 40.5 cm)**

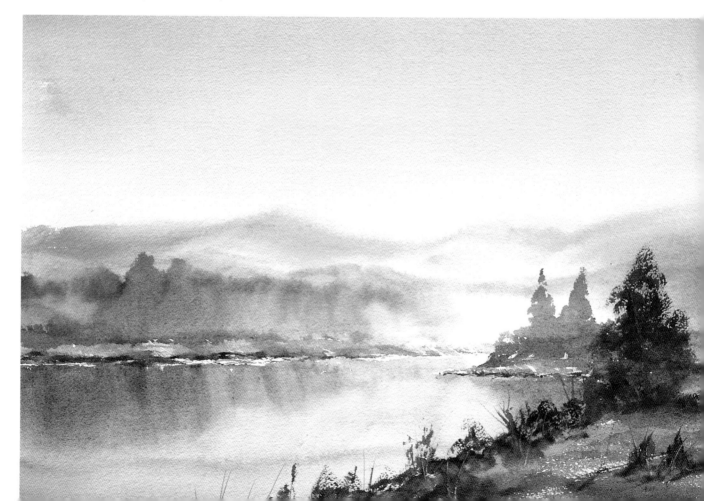

The River in Winter

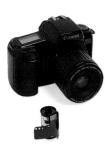

The combination of snow and water often makes for a dramatic painting, with the dark reflections of trees echoed by shadows thrown on the whiteness of snow. This demonstration shows how much color you can find in what might first seem a monochrome subject.

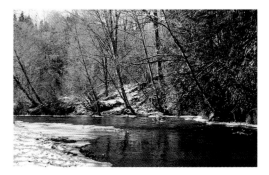

THE PHOTOGRAPH

There is plenty in this photograph to attract a watercolor artist, with the linearity of stark tree trunks juxtaposed against the horizontal planes of water and snow. The swirling water lends added interest, with some of the reflections broken and others more clearly defined.

THE PAINTING

The composition of the photo was good, so my main task was to add variation in color to background trees to avoid the monotony of too many grays and browns. To paint the water, I first put on an overall wash and while it was still wet dropped in reflected colors with rich paint and enjoyed watching them diffuse. Reflected trunks were put in just before the surface dried completely.

The River in Winter, 12 x 16" (30 x 40.5 cm)

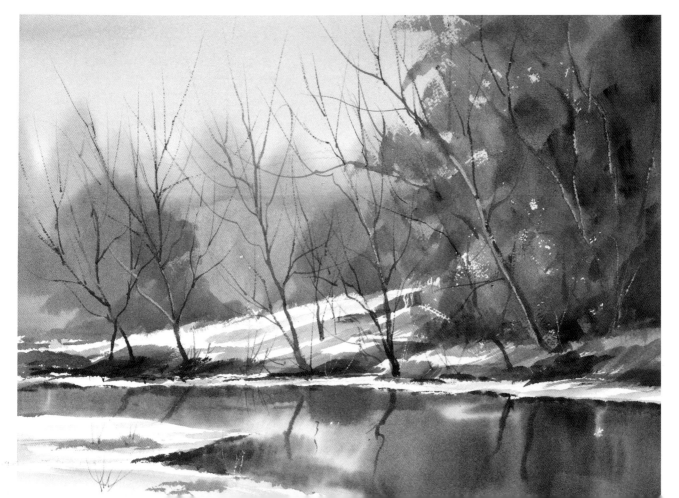

PROJECTS: Water

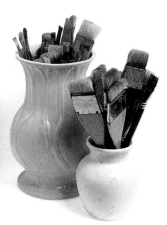

Water encompasses so many forms, from still, reflective surfaces to foaming waterfalls, that it presents a variety of challenges to the artist's technical capabilities, often within just one picture. Here I have picked photographs of the three types of water you will encounter most often: the relatively calm waters of an estuary; gently rolling waves on a seashore; and a fast-moving, rocky river. As usual, remember that your goal is to give a free interpretation of the scene and avoid falling into the trap of trying to reproduce every wave, reflection, and ripple. You can see my interpretations of these photographs on pages 120–2.

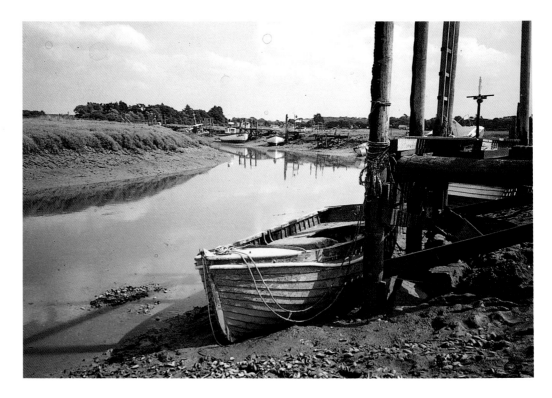

▲ *This photograph has a pleasing overall composition, albeit too heavy on one side. I also like its depth and tranquil atmosphere. However, the upright posts are distracting and there is nothing on the left to balance the mass of the boat and dock, so you will need to improve the composition. While the sky lacks interest, it offers you the chance to use cloud forms to provide balance. One of the main problems in this type of picture is avoiding monotony or muddiness in the dark dock structure. One method is to use various mixes of blues, browns, and light red. The beach also needs varying colors. Try for translucent shadows, allowing the underlying color to show through.*

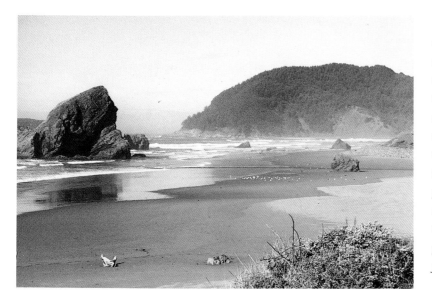

◄ *I took this photograph during one of my workshops on the California coast. I feel that the scene needs unification, so try overlapping the main rock against the background hill to pull things together. You might also wish to introduce a figure or two to lend scale and human interest, but take care where you position them or they will distract attention from the rock, which is the main focus of interest. Remember to put plenty of color into the foreground beach.*

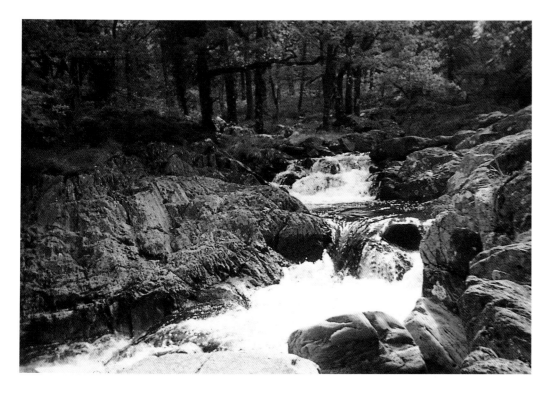

▲ *I took this exciting photograph in North Wales. The star of the scene is foaming white water, so avoid leaving white paper anywhere else or you will detract from its impact. The rocks in the immediate foreground should be separated in order to allow perspective on the river. Introduce as much color into the rocks as possible, experimenting with blues, browns, and ochres. Don't be too influenced by the relatively uniform color in the photograph or you will limit yourself. Never try to describe rocks such as these stone by stone. What you are after is the overall effect.*

FLOWERS

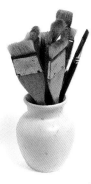

Of all the subjects covered in the book, flower paintings probably give you the most control over the design and composition of your photographs. You'll probably photograph your floral arrangements indoors, so you won't have to contend with the intrusions that often go with the territory in landscape photography—telephone poles, wires, and the like, nor will you be soaked by rainstorms or frozen in snow, so this will be your chance to concentrate on producing a really good photograph.

SETTING THE SCENE

It won't do to stick some flowers in a vase and take a snapshot. You must design your setting. Think of the background, the surface, the container, and, most important, the lighting.

Look for harmony of color in the flowers, particularly in a formal arrangement. Remember to consider the proportion of flowers to container as well as the type of container. Choose little jars or glasses for such small wild flowers as primroses, and stylishly shaped vases to echo the elegance of long-stemmed roses. Baskets, coffee pots, and jugs can all be pressed into service, as long as they are right for the flowers they are going to contain. However, don't allow the container to dominate. The stars of this scene are the flowers.

In arranging your flowers in their container, try for a natural look. They don't need to be perfectly balanced, but you will obviously not want them to look as if they are about to topple over. Don't position your flowers so that the light hits them all equally—in strong light they may look flat, and in shade they will appear dull. Arrange lighting that will illuminate some flowers while leaving others in shadow.

To get the best effect from your floral paintings, you need to keep both the background and surface undemanding. Anything you put in must enhance your flowers, not distract from them. Backgrounds can vary in tone, enabling you to put light flowers against a dark part of the background and vice versa. A reflective surface such as a polished table can be used to unify the painting.

Once you have decided on your flowers, lighting, container, surface, and background, consider whether or not another object on the surface might enhance your composition. Perhaps a book or favorite piece of driftwood carefully positioned might be just what is needed.

APPLYING DESIGN PRINCIPLES

Now, take a careful look through the viewfinder of your camera and make sure that you have applied the principles of design to your floral scene. Aim for informal balance between the flowers and the surrounding objects. The worst mistake you can make is to position your flowers in the exact center of the scene. Move them to one side, using a less dominant object for balance. The

**Iris and Jasmine,
11 x 8½"
(28 x 21.5 cm)**
I loved the deep, rich blue of these irises against the purity of the white jasmine. In a loose, fresh watercolor, the aim is always to convey a general impression of the flowers rather than to execute a tight copy of each blossom. I could have masked out the jasmine before starting to paint, but felt that in this case, using white gouache would work better. The rigger brush is ideal for painting fine stems.

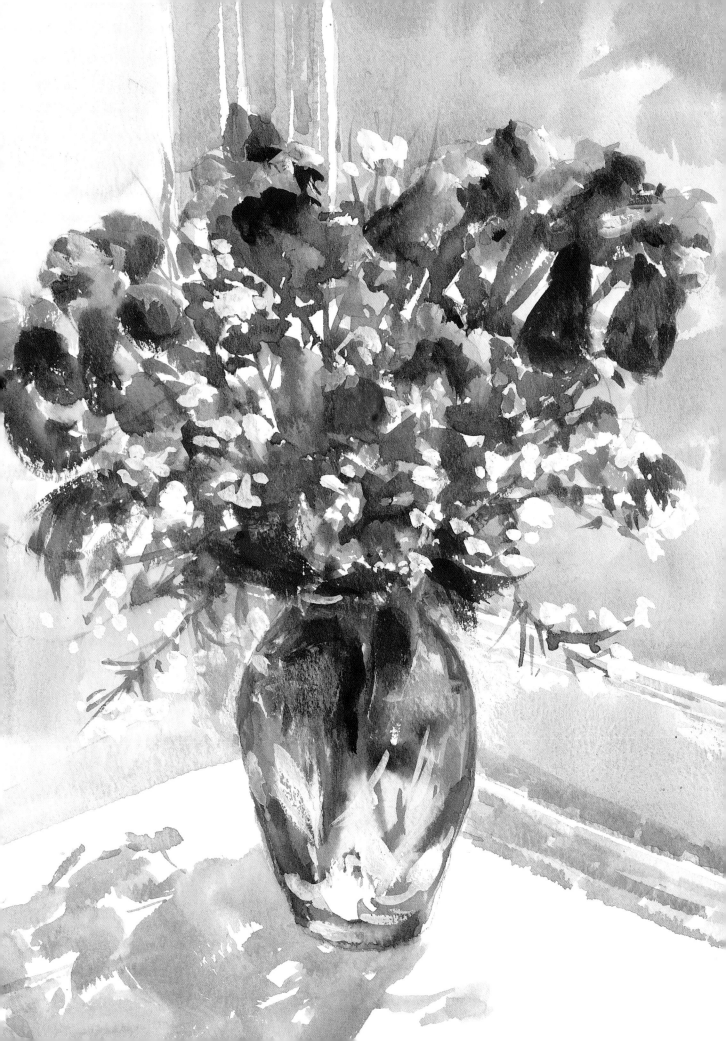

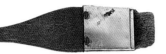

▼ *Below are four colors that are particularly useful for floral paintings, shown full strength and watered down.*

permanent mauve

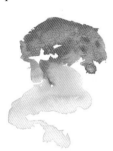

cadmium orange

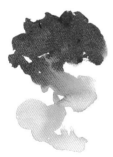

permanent rose

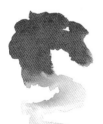

cadmium red

thought that you put into creating your floral scenes is all good practice for general design.

EXPERIMENTING WITH COLOR

Once you have a perfectly composed photograph, you have to start the thinking process all over again. You are not attempting here to produce perfect botanical specimens with every petal and stamen in place, but to paint a free, lively watercolor that will capture the freshness and beauty of the flowers in your arrangement.

One thing I find helpful in this respect is to use an oval mop brush with a good point, which allows for delicacy without encouraging overworking. The hake comes into its own again for backgrounds and surfaces, while the rigger is reserved for stems and delicate foliage. I stay mainly with my seven usual colors (see page 13), but sometimes add cadmium orange, cadmium red, permanent mauve, and permanent rose to my palette.

▲ *Here you can see the effect of first dampening the paper and then dropping in various pigments that are allowed to intermingle with one another. This might be a good way in which to start your floral painting, introducing stronger, richer color as the paper dries.*

All the principles of design apply as much to this subject as to any other, but there is room for a little experimentation, too. Perhaps you might try wetting your paper first, then dropping in areas of color, letting them blend. As the paper dries, indicate some hard edges to show the margin of a petal or leaf. Even when you are working from the most beautifully composed photograph you will find areas that need careful counterbalance, such as putting light flowers against dark foliage and darker flowers and leaves against a light background. Compare colors and tones against each other; a red dahlia may be darker in tone than a mauve aster next to it, for example.

Your overall principles should be to paint your floral scenes using a minimum number of brushstrokes and seeing the flowers as patches of color, rather than arrangements of petals. This will portray the freshness, delicacy, and beauty of your flowers better than a photograph ever could.

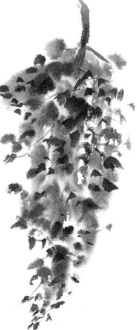

◄ *Here the method of dropping pigments in to damp paper is shown in practice. The color was dropped in wet-into-wet and allowed to diffuse. As the paper dried, strong, sharp strokes were introduced, using the pigment almost undiluted.*

Bluebell Wood

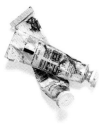

Although flowers in the wild don't allow you the same opportunity as indoor arrangements to compose a perfect photograph, there is something special about their quality growing in their own habitat, which makes for a lovely painting.

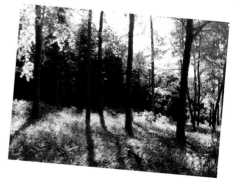

THE PHOTOGRAPH

I couldn't resist taking a photograph of these bluebell woods near my home; the swathe of color beneath the trees each spring is always a delight. Woodland photographs can be tricky because shafts of light shining between the trees can mislead the camera's light meter. Also, you will often have to include more tree trunks than you will wish to put in your painting.

THE PAINTING

The challenge was to convey the massed flowers without overworking. The most difficult part was the foreground, with its mixture of greens and blues. I changed the lighting to give more interest to the tree trunks, and pared down the number of trees. The figure of the little girl adds life and provides a center of interest.

***Bluebell Wood,* 10½ x 15" (27 x 38 cm)**

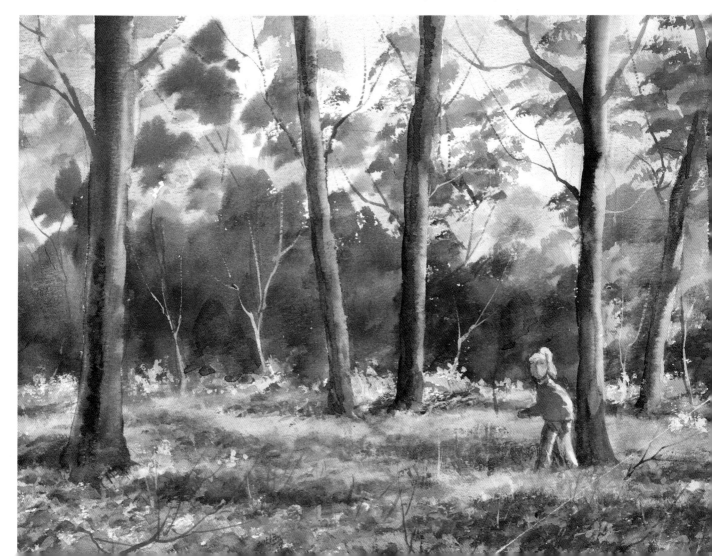

Yellow Roses

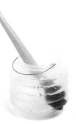

This is an example of the way my "fast and loose" techniques can be applied to painting flowers. No attempt is made to be botanically correct. The aim is to produce a free, fresh painting, pleasing to artist and viewer, giving a good general impression of the floral arrangement.

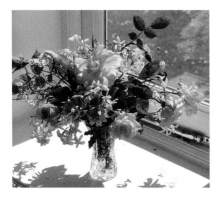

THE PHOTOGRAPH

This charmingly informal little floral arrangement was well beyond its peak of perfection, but I thought that it would make a good subject for a fast, loose painting, so I decided to photograph it anyway. I took three photographs, placing the vase experimentally in different lights, such as in front of a window and in full sunlight on a garden path. The photograph in which the flowers were illuminated strongly on one side by window light seemed to me the most satisfactory of the three. In arranging the flowers, I aimed to get as much contrast as possible between the light tones of the yellow blossoms and the darker leaves.

THE PAINTING

The temptation with a subject such as this is to try to copy every leaf and petal, which would produce much too controlled and rigid a painting. I merely sketch in the generic shapes of flowers, allowing myself a lot of freedom of expression as I work. I paint quickly, using my oval mop brush, and put in plenty of value contrast to produce sparkle in my finished painting. Individual rose petals are merely hinted at, using the point of the oval mop. The more economically they are portrayed, the livelier they will look.

Yellow Roses,
**8 x 9"
(20.5 x 23 cm)**

Sunlit Daffodils

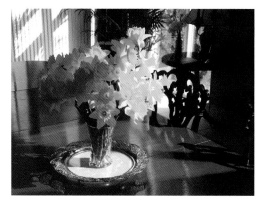

As in all my floral paintings, my aim here was to express the essence and color of daffofils without attempting to paint each one individually.

THE PHOTOGRAPH

This photograph was taken at home in my dining room. The dark, shiny table made a good foil for the bright yellow of the flowers. I emphasized this contrast by using strong daylight from the window coming in from the right. I also wanted to convey an impression of some other items in the room, such as a distant lamp and a potted palm. I decided that standing the vase of flowers on a small silver tray would give a more formal air to the arrangement, in keeping with the setting.

THE PAINTING

When I looked at the photo, it was evident that the complex shape of the chairs was a distraction, so I left them out of my painting. The potted palm and lamp were merely hinted at, while the tabletop was painted wet-into-wet, using a medley of colors. Rich surrounding dark values point up the joyful color of the daffodils and give them form and substance. Again, no attempt was made to render individual petals. The overall shape of the arrangement, with the suggestion of a trumpet here and there, clearly identifies the flowers as daffodils.

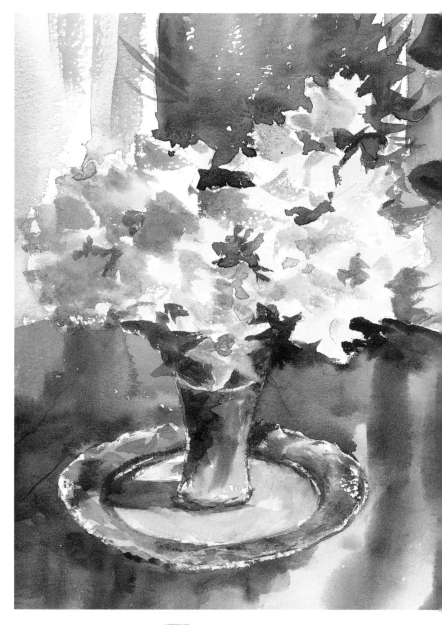

Sunlit Daffodils, 9½ x 7½" (24 x 19 cm)

PROJECTS: Flowers

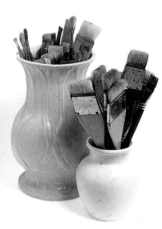

Permit me to emphasize again that when painting from photos of flowers, it's even more important than with most other subjects to avoid trying to replicate every detail. It simply won't work. Do just a rough pencil sketch of the general floral arrangement. If you get too detailed, you'll tighten up too much when you move on to the painting stage. Make use of the hard and soft edges that are characteristic of floral subjects. Employing strong value contrasts is another important principle to apply; placing light flowers against dark leaves or backgrounds and vice versa will bring your paintings to life. See my interpretations of these photos on pages 123–4.

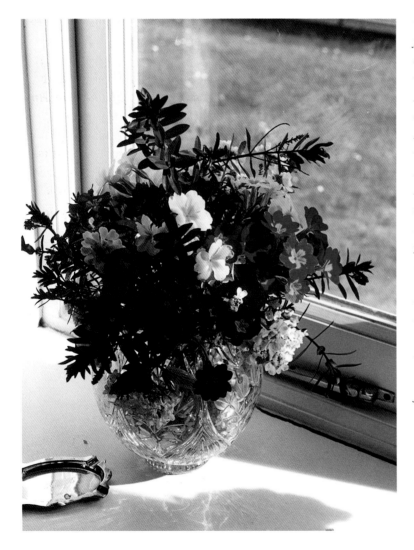

◄ *There is so much variation of strong floral color in this photograph, you may be tempted to be too precise in your rendition of individual blossoms. Remember, instead, that fresh and loose brushstrokes will give your painting life. Lighten the flowers nearest the camera, which in the photograph are so dark that they can hardly be distinguished. If you were to reproduce this photo as is in your value sketch, you would see that it would make for an unbalanced painting. Adding a few extra flowers on the left side will also contribute balance. With the ashtray, glass vase, and window, there is plenty of reflection in this picture—but don't be tempted to convey the cut-glass effect of the vase; it would distract the eye from the flowers. Keep your interpretation free to give just an impression of the lightness and airiness inherent in such reflective surfaces.*

▶ *I took this photograph because I loved the effect of the bright colors of the roses playing against the rich, dark tonality of the leaves. Try painting this on a wet-into-wet background, gradually using stronger and richer color as the paper dries. Remember that you only need to indicate the petals of the roses with economy of stroke. The best way to handle the clear glass vase is to repeat some of the color from the foliage to give the painting unity.*

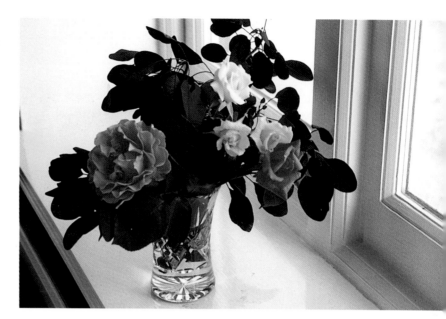

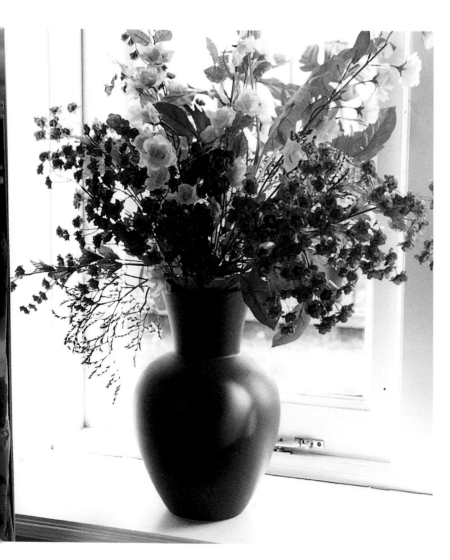

◀ *When I saw this beautiful, richly colored vase in a shop, I couldn't resist buying it. At home I filled it with a variety of silk flowers that have a particularly lifelike look. Any painting inspired by this photo should convey an impression of numerous small blossoms. Use a wet-into-wet technique, with rigger work and stronger color added once the paper has dried. You will need to work fast and decisively.*

FIGURES IN THE LANDSCAPE

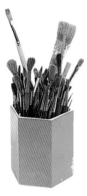

When you look at a watercolor scene, you may often have a feeling that something is missing. Then you realize that what is lacking is a figure, either human or animal. Scenes of boatyards, beaches, streets, and markets all look rather desolate without figures—which is fine if that is the intended effect, but it's more likely that the artist may have been afraid of spoiling the landscape by adding figures.

LEARNING TO PAINT FIGURES

You don't need life-drawing classes to learn how to paint figures in a landscape, but you do need to follow a few simple rules, and you do need to practice. Next time you're out with your camera, take some shots that include people or animals. Also have your sketchbook along and jot down quick people impressions. Don't bother with details. Just concentrate on movement, areas of light and dark, and link your figures together in pairs or groups. Even if the photo reference you use doesn't have figures in it, put them in your painting if you feel they are needed. They'll add life, movement, scale, and variety. Figures can also become the focal point of a scene, but if they are featured, place them off-center, at a different distance from each edge of your painting.

SCALE AND VALUE CONTRAST

Figure size is important, of course, and many students seem to find scale a problem. It's all a question of placement. A figure of a certain size placed in the foreground would look ridiculously small, but put that same-sized figure farther back, and it would look like a giant. One way to overcome this problem is to draw the figure on tracing paper, then move it around your drawing until it looks right. If your figure is near a doorway or a rowboat, scale is fairly straightforward. The figure shouldn't have to get down on hands and knees to get through the door, and must be the right size to sit in the rowboat.

Make sure to place light figures against a dark background or vice versa. Use the device of painting dark trousers and white shirt against light and dark backgrounds respectively for effective value contrast.

KEEP IT ECONOMICAL

Once you've become used to putting figures in your paintings, you'll be surprised how little work you need to do on them as long as the basic proportions are right. In a café scene, for instance, a few colorful splashes under an awning, accompanied by a few strokes for legs, is sufficient. Your viewers will fill in the rest for themselves. It may encourage you to know that an artist friend of mine used to avoid adding figures to his paintings. Having once discovered just how simply

Cliff Path, Kalymnos,
(14 x 11')
35.5 x 28 cm
There were no figures in the photograph I used as reference for this painting. I added them to draw the eye of the viewer into the picture, placing the tops of the figures against a dark background. The distant rocky cliffs needed to be out of focus, so I painted them wet-into-wet, using combinations of light red, ultramarine and raw sienna. I put in more contrast and warmer, richer colors as I moved forward in the scene.

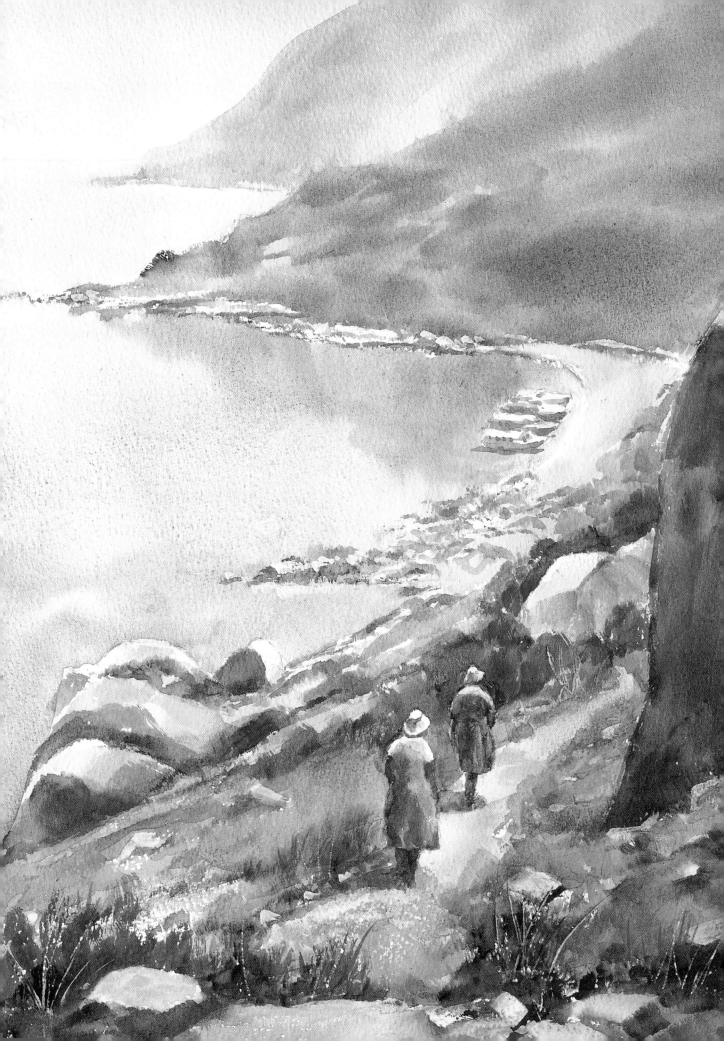

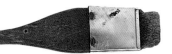

and economically they could be indicated, he now seeks out populated scenes, which he portrays with tremendous vigor and simplicity.

The problem many students need to overcome is their fear of painting figures. A few days with a sketchpad should convince you that simply drawn figures are easy to include, and will contribute to building livelier and more authentic paintings.

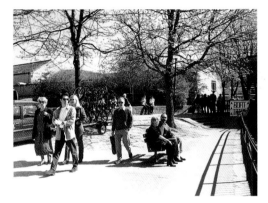

A photograph of an everyday scene in town can be a very useful reference when adding figures to a landscape painting. Figures can be transplanted to any scene that requires some human interest.

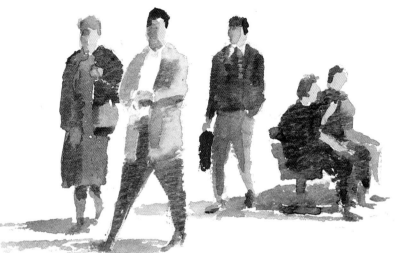

Here, I have extracted a few figures from the scene on the left and moved them around. I've also simplified them; putting features on faces, for example, is not necessary.

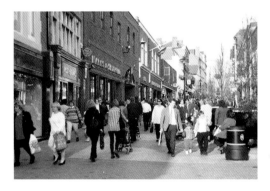

This is a typical urban scene of a busy street, with families out and about doing their shopping. Notice the proportions of figures in relation to the buildings.

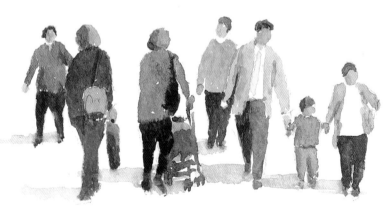

The people in this scene have been drawn direct from the photograph on the left. Even with no background, the viewer would guess that they are in urban surroundings.

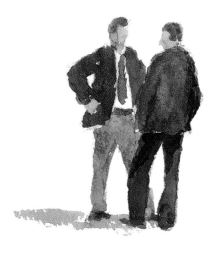

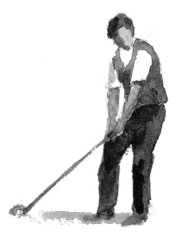

Notice how shadows are used to anchor figures on the ground and link them with one another.
In the countryside, figures engaged in rural tasks and leisure activities are good to photograph for future reference.

TIPS FOR PAINTING FIGURES

Do keep your figures simple. They can be very roughly indicated as long as the proportions are right.

Do keep heads small and bodies long and lean.

Do make your figures an integral part of the scene.

Do forget about detailing feet. They are not usually necessary at all.

Do give shadows to your figures whenever possible. They help to anchor them.

Do remember value contrast and scale.

Don't put your figure or group of figures in the middle of a painting.

Don't forget to make a pair or group of figures a single unit, with a single shadow.

Don't make your figures stand at attention. Give them a natural stance.

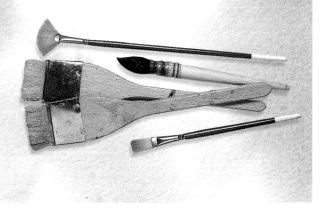

Market Square in Orta, Italy

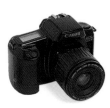

An urban scene that would be static if uninhabited springs to life once some human figures are included. This demonstration shows that even lightly suggested figures are enough to make a crucial difference to the feel of the painting.

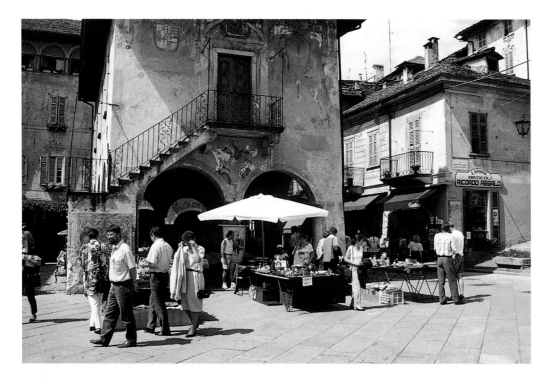

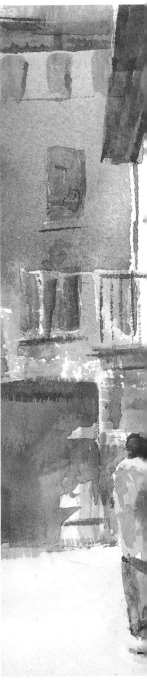

THE PHOTOGRAPH

This photograph of a street market was taken in the ancient town of Orta in Italy. It's a typical Mediterranean scene with mellowed buildings, shuttered windows, and people strolling between market stalls. I was sure it would make a pleasing composition for a watercolor, with hardly any alteration necessary. Notice that the foremost building has been framed off-center.

THE PAINTING

I made only minor changes, such as omitting the girl partly out of frame on the left and correcting the verticals on the building behind her. But apart from that, it was just a matter of simplifying the scene. Although the figures have been pared down to the essentials—indeed, only the foreground strollers even have feet—they still retain movement and purpose. The faded mural on the main building has been merely suggested by some areas of warmer color. This scene would lose all its vitality if the people were omitted.

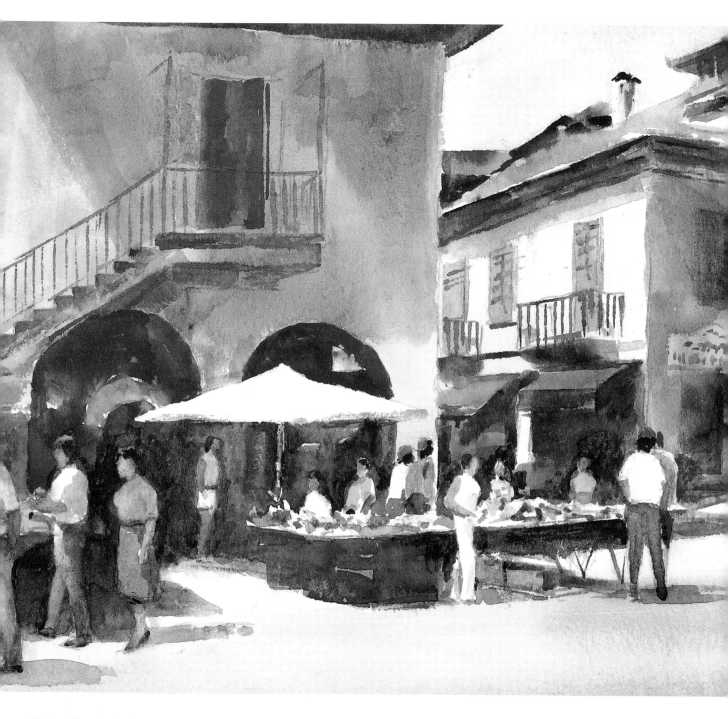

Market Square in Orta, Italy, 7½ x 11" (19 x 28 cm)

PROJECTS: Figures in the Landscape

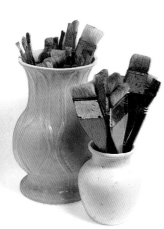

These photographs offer a variety of populated scenes to use as the basis for paintings that include figures. In this project, your whole objective is to simplify the image while still retaining its action and movement. This approach is advocated throughout the book, for even when painting static subjects such as flowers, the aim has been to express their freshness and life. As noted earlier, you can forget about painting facial features on your figures, and often you can even omit their feet. Think of people as part of the overall setting, not as add-ons using a different technique. My paintings from these photographs are on pages 124–5.

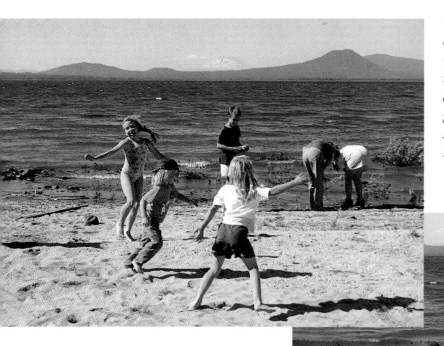

◀ *Each year, I set up camp in a beautiful spot in the mountains of Oregon with our large family. In this instance, grandchildren were running about wildly, so I snatched some hasty photographs of them. Your task here is to select some of the figures and transpose them into a painting.*

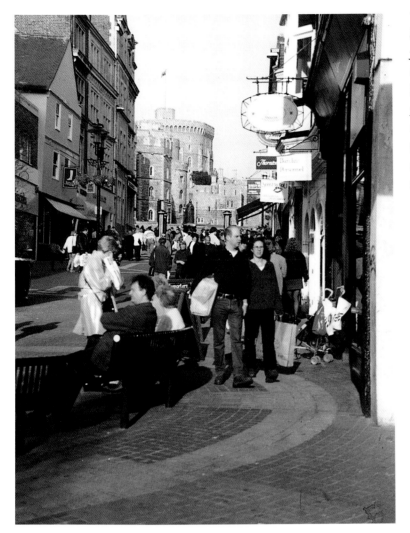

◄ *This is a photograph I took on a busy Saturday afternoon in Windsor; you can see the famous castle in the background. Your chief aim here must be to simplify the scene as much as possible, particularly the buildings themselves, by restricting yourself to using a 1"(25 mm) flat brush. You will be able to retain the bustling atmosphere by working with large, free brushstrokes.*

► *I took this photograph during one of my workshops in Venice. Try to convey the bustle and life of the scene without including too much detail. The yellow of the flowers will provide pleasing color in the foreground, which can be picked up again farther back in the scene. The figure of the man on the right is rather lost against the background—a problem you will need to address in your painting.*

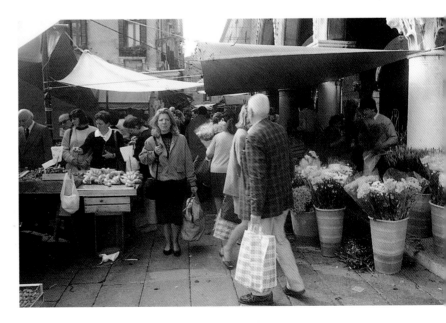

BUILDINGS

Many people who are able to produce loose, free watercolors of skies, trees, and water lose that sense of spontaneity and tighten up when it comes to buildings. While they would not attempt to describe every leaf in a woodland scene, being content to take viewers into partnership and allow them to do some of the work, they don't seem able to apply the same approach to buildings. Instead, they feel compelled to portray every window, door, even every brick—and the painting loses all vitality.

KEEP YOUR PAINTING FREE

I once took a group of painters to Venice for two weeks. The students included four architects who for the first week produced accurate and detailed drawings of the city. It was not until the second week that I convinced them that when using paint, it simply is not necessary to put in every structural detail. They also failed to establish an ambience of old warm stone of subtle colors. But once they got the message, they turned out loose, impressionistic paintings that captured the atmosphere of wonderful, ancient Venice.

I've never made a secret of the fact that I've been greatly influenced by the work of Edward Seago, and have spent many hours studying old exhibition catalogues of his paintings, marveling at the way he was able to suggest buildings, especially Venetian structures, with such economy and freedom. I've always tried to apply Seago's approach to my own watercolors, but sometimes I have to fight the urge to overwork.

One device that may help to keep your buildings loose and impressionistic is to limit your working time. Long painting sessions are more likely to result in very detailed work. Another is to restrict your brushes to large flat ones for such things as windows, roofs, chimneys, and balconies. These are the danger areas in terms of overworking. When I'm painting in Greece, I often indicate a whole village with a few brushstrokes of my 1" (25 mm) flat, and I employ this same technique when interpreting photos. The flat edge can be used for roofs and balconies; the corner of the brush for windows. Using a 1" brush positively prevents me from being too detailed. Lock your #2 sables away in a closet!

ADAPTING THE PHOTOGRAPH

This temptation to overwork a watercolor is probably at its strongest when you use photographs for reference. Having more time to put in unnecessary detail, you'll be inclined to copy colors from the photo as well. However, to avoid portraying boring buildings, you must use a good range of colors that would not be apparent in a photograph. One of the questions I'm frequently asked is: "What color should I mix

Back Canal in Venice,
14 x 11"
(40.5 x 28 cm)
The big challenge in this scene was to create the atmosphere and color of old buildings while avoiding the temptation to overwork them. I varied building color by using a hake brush before turning to my 25 mm (1") flat brush to add, very economically, architectural details such as doors and windows. Using this brush makes it almost impossible to belabor details such as individual bricks. The viewer's imagination will augment a scene as needed.

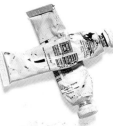

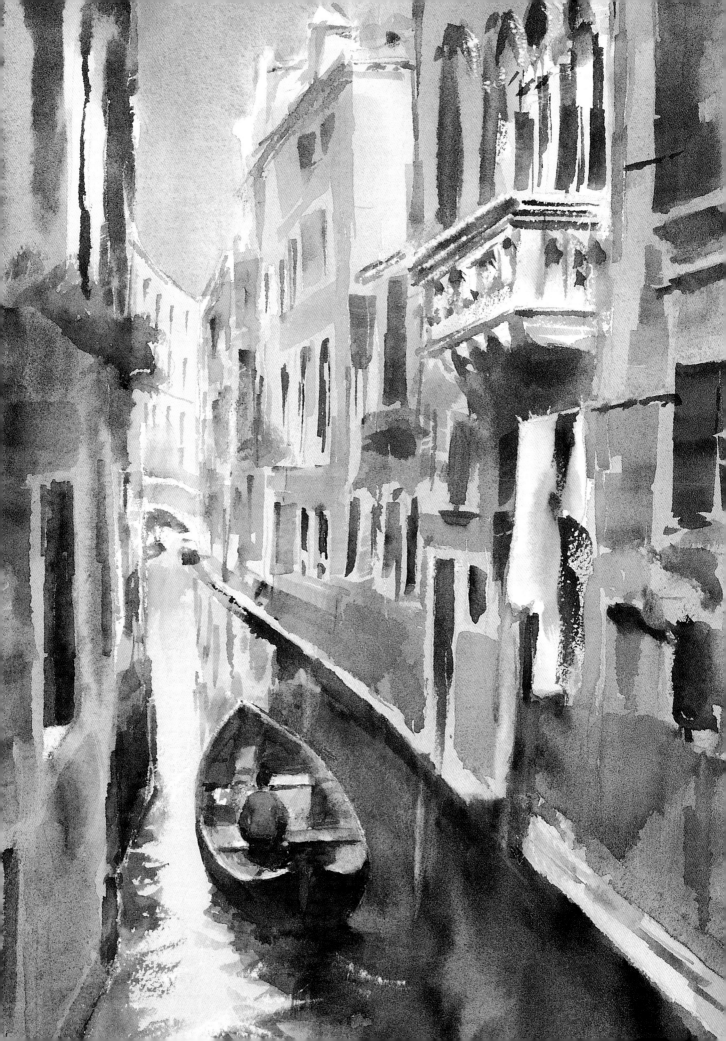

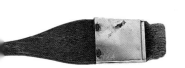

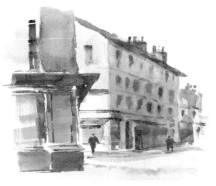

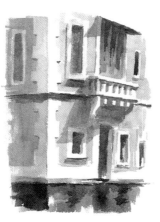

▲ *To convey a sense of distance, when painting a building, leave some windows out entirely and minimize others by indicating them only.*

▶ *Shadows on buildings are important for establishing surface shapes as well as forms. However, they must always be painted in a transparent and spontaneous way, allowing the original wall color to show through.*

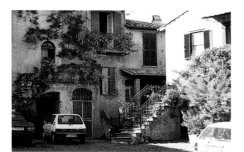

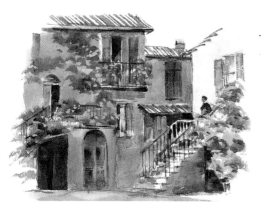

◀ *The little vignette below shows how you can take out cars, add people, and use foliage to soften a painting. Notice how I have attempted to get more color into the walls. The blue flowers were put in last, using white gouache mixed with ultramarine watercolor.*

for a local stone wall?" In fact, you add colors as you go along; blues, reds, browns, and ochres are all needed to produce the right effect.

The vertical lines of buildings are often distorted in photographs. This must be corrected in your drawing before you begin to paint. While a window need not be detailed, it must be straight. An important point I learned from Seago is to put in some windows before the paint on a building wall is dry. This creates an out-of-focus look that is very effective in distant buildings.

SHADOWS AND LIGHT

In photographs of buildings, you are likely to have strong shadows that appear opaque and dead. In a watercolor they must be transparent, showing the underlying hue. However, if a photograph taken on a dull day may not show much difference in the tones of various surfaces, which makes for a flat, boring picture. Your value sketch is where you correct this, dramatizing and harmonizing the lighting, adding shadows to make the picture more exciting. Exploit each shadow to describe the surfaces and planes it falls on, but simplify, organize, and exaggerate values in order to make them more obvious for your viewer.

It's best to paint all the walls of a building together, dropping in a darker transparent wash to the shadowed side after the first wash has dried. If you paint in dark and light areas separately, you'll end up with a patchwork effect. Another change often required is painting a darker sky against which the shapes of lighter buildings can be profiled.

Greek Island Village

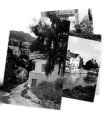

Your photographic viewpoint of buildings may often be blocked by trees, trucks, or building work. Take the photograph anyway, for, as this demonstration shows, it's easy to make adjustments when it comes to the painting.

THE PHOTOGRAPH

This scene was taken on a painting vacation in Kalymnos. The side of the road on the right seemed heavy and dead, with the dark wall and foliage providing a looming presence that detracted from the inviting feel of the simple white buildings.

THE VALUE SKETCH

In my value sketch, I corrected the imbalance by lightening the wall and reducing the weight of the foliage. I made the balcony on the house to the left the focal point by putting some figures on it, and used the perspective of the wall on the right to point to it.

THE PAINTING

I needed more skyline to define the terrain, and I also wanted to get as much color as possible into the barren hillside. I followed the changes made in my value sketch to lighten up the whole picture on the right. Finally, notice the variety of color I gave to the white walls.

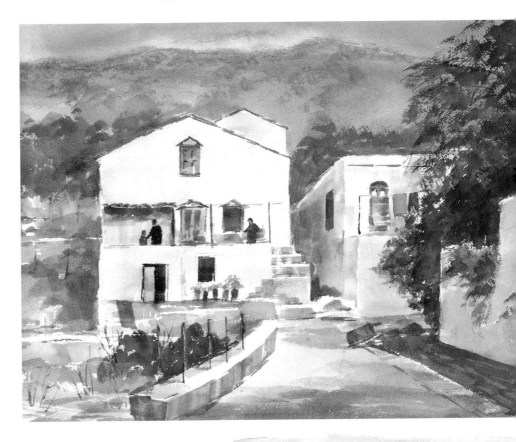

Greek Island Village,
12 x 16" (30 x 40.5 cm)

Market Cross at Malmesbury

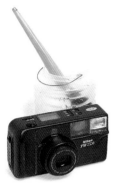

In many English towns, you can find old buildings islanded in the midst of modern life. While the temptation may be to eliminate the new, the danger is that you may produce a "candy box" painting. Instead, opt for a selective view that celebrates the old while presenting a truthful picture of the scene.

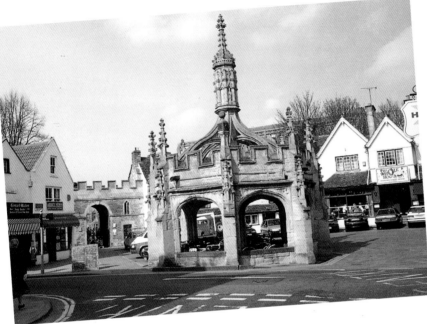

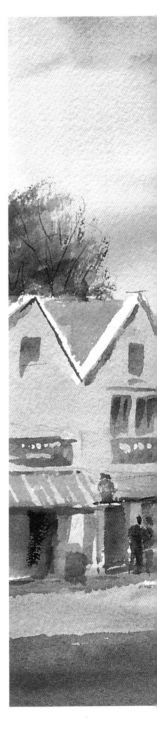

THE PHOTOGRAPH

I took this shot during one of my workshops in this delightful old town in Wiltshire. While the relation of the buildings to one another makes a satisfactory composition, there are intrusive details that distract atttention from the structure that is the main focal point of the picture.

THE PAINTING

Although the elaborate structure seems a complex subject to paint, I've managed to give a good general impression of it without too much detail by using the edge and corner of a 1" (25 mm) flat brush. While wanting to preserve the liveliness of the scene, I cut out some of the modern paraphernalia of cars, white and yellow lines on the road, and the blackboard menu for the restaurant. It often helps to add a few touches of bright color just for fun, and cars can usually provide that, so I did include a few, indicating them very simply. I decided to add more clouds to the sky, and also put in a few very loose figures to animate the scene.

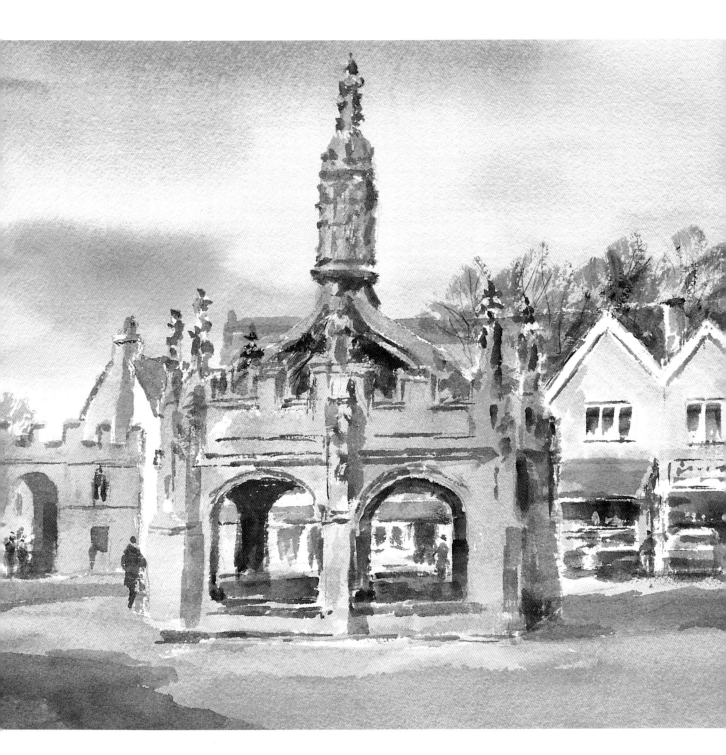

Market Cross at Malmesbury, 10 x 12" (25.5 x 30 cm)

The Hill in Orta, Italy

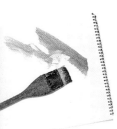

Tiled roofs and cobblestone streets are appealing to see as you wander around a town, and they make interesting accents in photographs. But in an impressionistic watercolor, I find it best to eliminate such details and just suggest their textures.

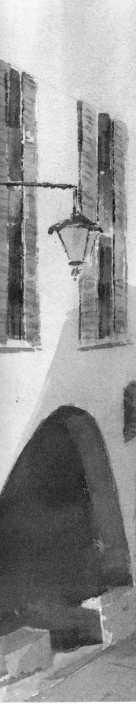

THE PHOTOGRAPH

I spent two weeks teaching in this lovely old town facing a lake, and took a number of photographs of its quaint cobbled streets with their mellowed buildings bright with pot plants. The contrast of light and shade here has confused the camera's light meter so both sky and water have been bleached almost to white, losing some of the charm of the view down the street.

THE PAINTING

More color was needed here than is apparent in the photograph, even in the shadowy area on the right. The eye is directed down the hill to the distant lake, so I've removed the distracting figure of the woman coming out of her gate on the right and contrasted the sunlit house against the lake, which in the painting has regained the blue reflected from the sky. It's easy with this type of scene to become distracted by cobblestones and roof tiles and miss the heart of the picture, so just suggest rough surfaces instead of detailing them. Notice that for balance and added interest, I've added a couple of windows to the house on the right, which had been blocked up in the photograph.

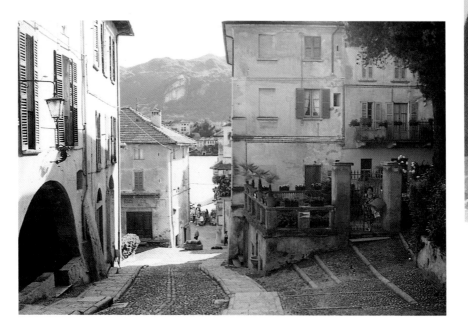

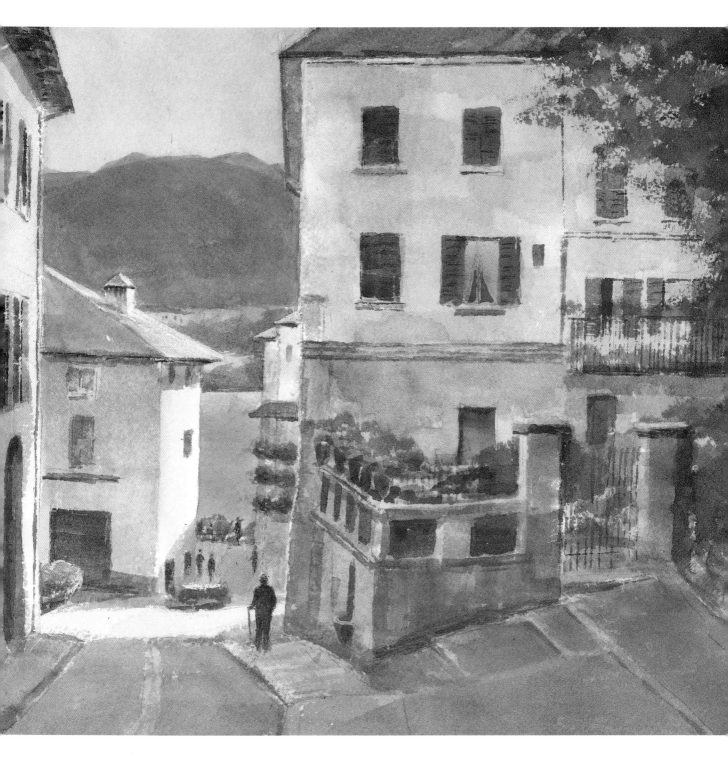

The Hill in Orta, Italy, 10 x 12" (25.5 x 30 cm)

PROJECTS: Buildings

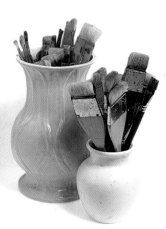

A 1" (25 mm) flat brush is your best ally in achieving a free, fresh approach to the painting of buildings, helping you to avoid the temptation of putting in too much detail. Be sure to get more varied color into the walls than you see in these photographs. Otherwise, your paintings will look dead. The flat, uniform color that you take for granted in a photograph doesn't hold its own in a watercolor. Remember always to do value sketches before embarking upon your final paintings. Make any changes there that you feel will enhance your composition. This is also your chance to improve value contrasts to give your paintings good definition and visual interest. You can find my interpretations of these photographs on pages 126–7.

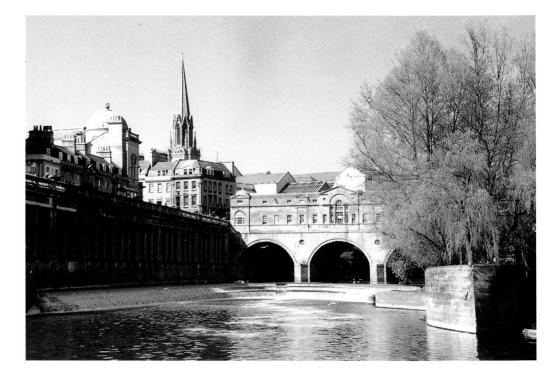

▲ *I took this photograph on a beautiful sunny morning in Bath, England, noted for the glorious color of its stonework. Your task here is to convey the busy architecture without becoming bogged down in too much detail. Try putting in windows using just the corner of your large brush. You will probably need to mask out the church steeple. The trees on the right provide a good foil of soft, free texture against the architecture of the bridge. The hake and rigger brushes should be used in portraying the tree.*

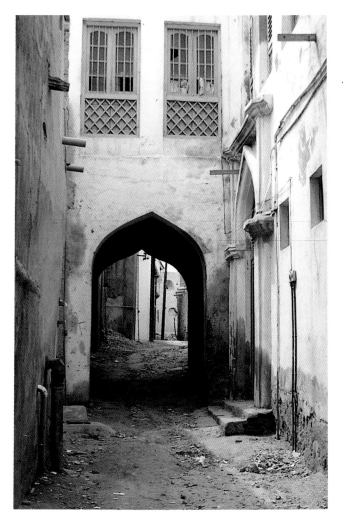

◀ *I was asked to run a painting course in Muscat, Oman, and this photograph was taken in one of the city's narrow back streets. Your first thought on how to translate this into a successful watercolor painting should be to put more varied color into the walls and ground. Sticking faithfully to the colors in the photography would produce a dull painting. A robed figure might be a good addition to give human interest to the scene—but remember to take great care as regards the position and scale of the figure. Try to retain the atmosphere of antiquity in your painting.*

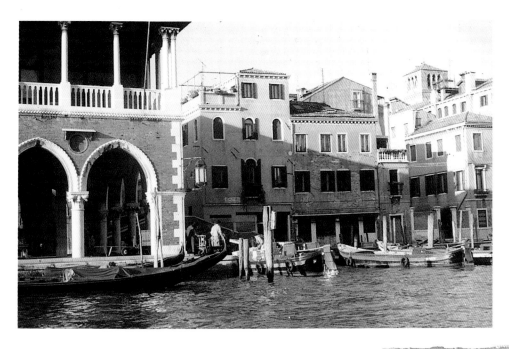

◀ *This is a corner of Venice's fish market. You will need to convey its bustle and color, perhaps by adding more activity; the photograph was taken at a quiet time of the day. Elaborate architecture must be painted in the simplest possible way. The water could be made more interesting by adding reflections and the sky darkened to give the buildings a stronger profile.*

THE FOUR SEASONS

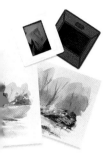

This chapter is something of a new challenge, because what I'm asking you to do here is to change the season portrayed in your photograph to quite another in your painting. You can choose to turn winter to summer, autumn to spring—whatever appeals to your imagination. It will mean altering the whole color scheme and atmosphere of your painting— quite a tricky enterprise. Finding the skeleton of a winter tree beneath the enveloping leaf canopy of a summer one can be downright difficult.

Here and on the following pages are examples of my own to set you off on the right track. Don't be daunted by these exercises; they can be great fun to do. More than ever, always do a value sketch before embarking on a painting in which you change the seasons, because the whole pattern of the scene may need to be altered.

CHANGING THE PALETTE
In summer and spring, you'll generally need a varying range of greens: cool blue-greens in the background and warm yellow-greens in the foreground. Autumn distant trees require mauves, and for closer foliage, employ light reds and browns. In winter, distant trees become subtle grays, with a stronger mix of browns and blues coming in as you move toward the foreground.

Snow scenes are great fun to paint. You'll have a much stronger, more

contrasting pattern to your picture, with shadows being mainly blue on the paper-white snow. Winter scenes require plenty of practice with the rigger for authentic portrayal of delicate bare branches and twigs.

SUBTLE SEASONS
Autumn and winter are seasons when you can use the subtle effects of mist to create atmosphere. Here, of course, the tones of different layers of the landscape vary even more. While foreground objects will be dark and crisp, anything in the background should be painted wet-into-wet, employing subtle tones. The whole process gives you a real chance to exercise your imagination, and you'll be surprised at the interesting effects that result.

Woodland Stream, 16 x 12" (40.5 x 30 cm)
I photographed this English woodland scene in Devon in summer (below). When I decided to paint it, I changed the season to winter and made it a cold, misty day. The colors therefore needed to be changed from various greens to grays, browns, and mauves. Mist is an ideal subject for watercolor as it lends itself so well to wet-into-wet treatment.

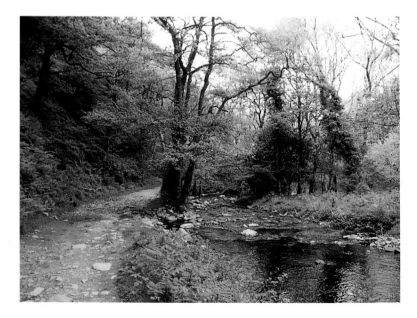

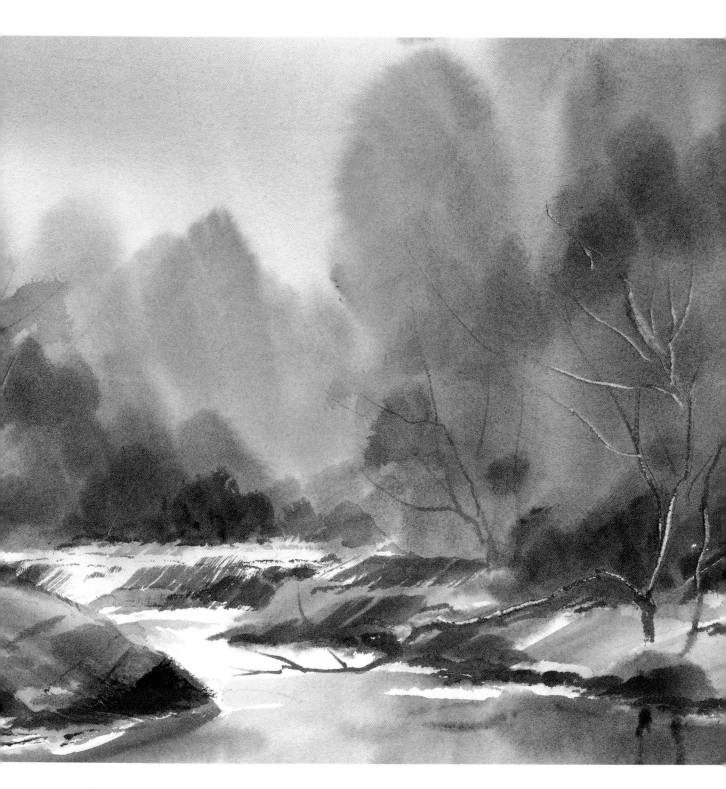

River Mist, 12 x 16" (30 x 40.5 cm)

Shadows Across the Lane

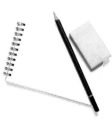

Within a few weeks, the changing of one season to another can cause a scene to look radically different from the one you have photographed. When you paint from your imagination, think about the alteration that the landscape has undergone.

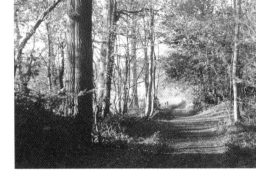

Shadows Across the Lane—Autumn,
12 x 16"
(30 x 40.5 cm)

THE PHOTOGRAPH

Every autumn in England, I used to teach at Phillips House, a lovely mansion near Salisbury, Wiltshire. I took this photo on one of my early-morning walks there. The sun cast long tree shadows that formed a dramatic pattern across the tiny lane. I deliberately picked a viewpoint in which one tree is dominant.

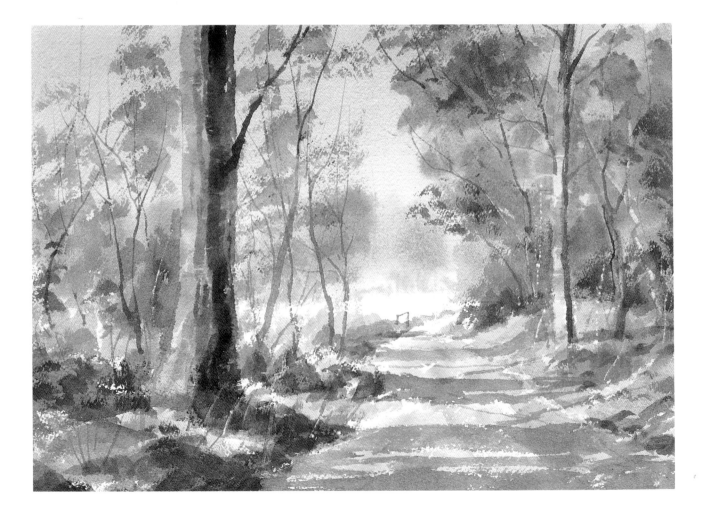

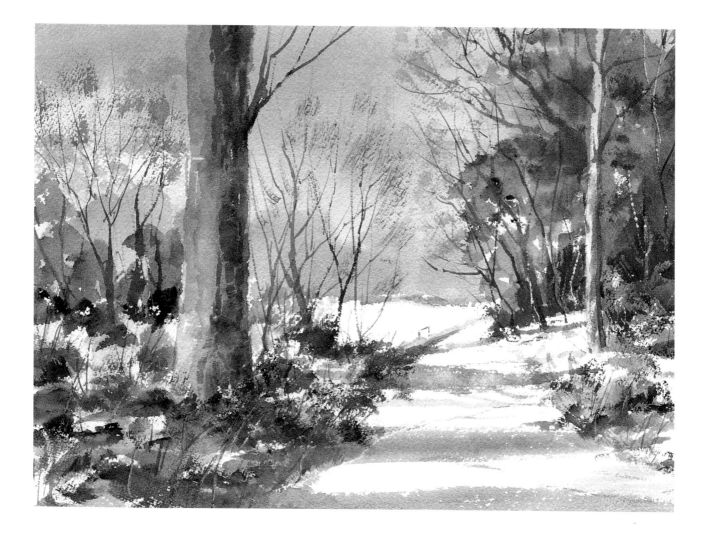

THE PAINTINGS

As you can see, I have made very few changes from the photograph in the painting on the left. By softening the background, I've given the scene more distance to the end of the lane, drawing the viewer into the picture. The shadows stretching across the lane enhance a feeling of sunshine in the scene.

In the painting above, I have imagined the whole scene under snow. With leaves off the trees, much more rigger work was required to depict their skeletal branches. You will notice that I have softened the shadows and made them more blue, rather than the mauve I used in the autumnal painting. I decided to add yellow to the sky, while the ground was left mainly as untouched paper with just a hint of yellow to reflect the sky and thus retain unity in the picture.

My aim in both of these pictures was to capture the atmosphere of peace and quiet of a scene that always brings back many happy memories.

Shadows Across the Lane—Winter,
12 x 16"
(30 x 40.5 cm)

Bigsweir Bridge

If you are particularly fond of a local view, you'll probably find that you paint it repeatedly at different times of year, enjoying its nuances as seasons and weather conditions change. However, working from imagination only is excellent practice.

THE PHOTOGRAPH

For twenty-five years, I lived at the very top of a distant hill that looks down on a bridge spanning a slow-moving river way below. This photograph was taken in very poor light in winter, so the overall effect is rather dull and monochromatic. Indeed, it could almost be mistaken for a black-and-white photograph.

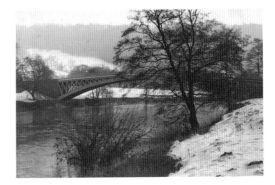

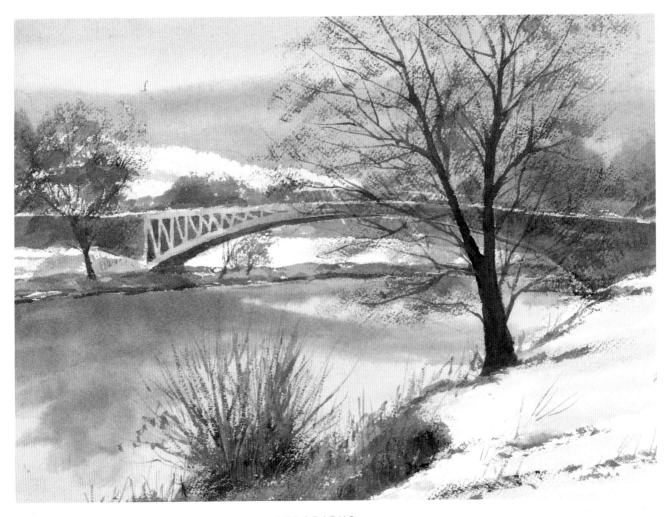

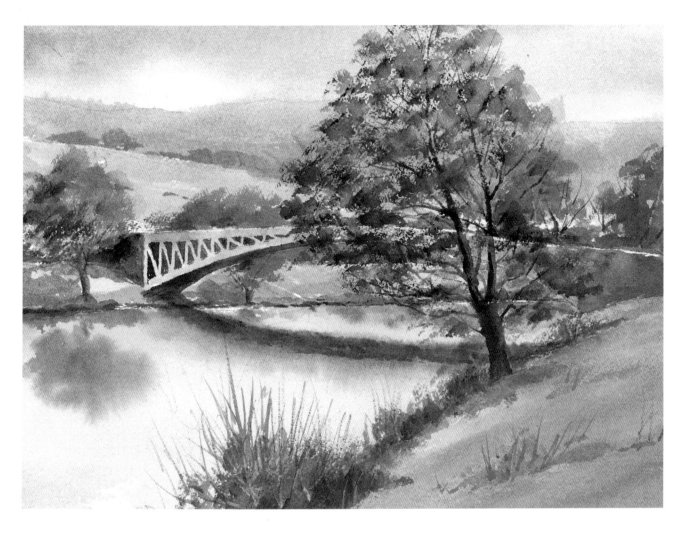

THE PAINTINGS

In my winter painting, I have increased value contrasts and colors considerably. I love the spot and have painted it several times, but always found the bridge girders difficult to describe convincingly in a loose watercolor. In fact, here I've managed to avoid them altogether on the right-hand side of the bridge. Notice the high waterline on the banks where the snow has been washed away.

In my second painting, I've referred to the same photograph but this time turned the scene into summer, using various greens, with a full-leaf canopy on the trees. This exercise requires a good deal of thought and imagination but is very rewarding. As always, the river color is a reflection of the sky. Greens change from the cool blue-greens of distant hills to warmer foreground colors to create a feeling of depth.

Bigsweir Bridge—Summer,
**9½ x 13"
(24 x 33 cm)**

Bigsweir Bridge—Winter,
9½ x 13" (24 x 33 cm)

GALLERY

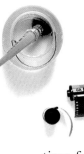

Traveling the world to teach watercolor painting gives me opportunities to see many different types of landscape. The drawback is that there are never enough hours to paint them! But there is always time for some photography, and when I arrive home in England, I have numerous rolls of film.

Not all my photos will be suitable as painting reference, but I try to return each time with a higher proportion of usable pictures. Looking back at some taken a decade ago, I'm horrified at how little thought I once put into photo composition. As you make a practice of considering composition for paintings, you'll find, as I have, that you automatically begin to frame your reference photographs with more care.

The demonstrations in this book all include photographs to use as a basis for paintings. In this chapter, I'll show you what I had in mind when I took those photos. I've made several changes in my finished paintings to intensify the original image and atmosphere. Study the design and color changes I've made and compare my paintings with the ones you've created based on my photos. This final exercise will draw together all the threads of the book.

Haystack Rock, Oregon
12 x 16"
(30 x 40.5 cm)
While I needed to do little to the general design here, I made value changes, added sea mist below the distant hills, and generally tried to vary the colors. I reflected the yellow of the sky into the sea and pools on the beach to add interest and unity.

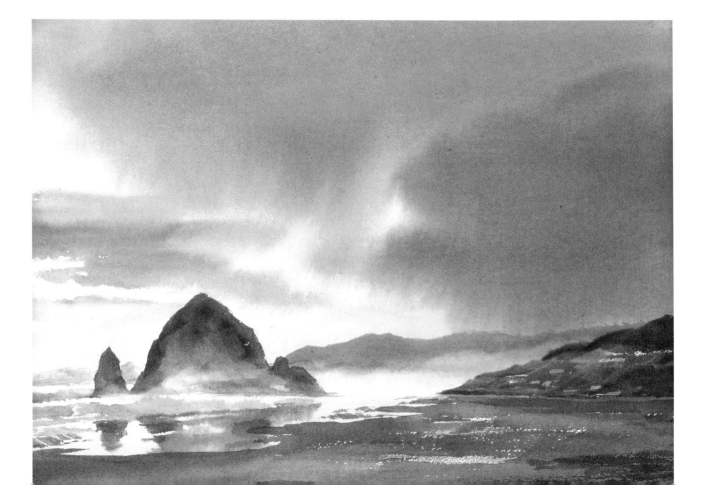

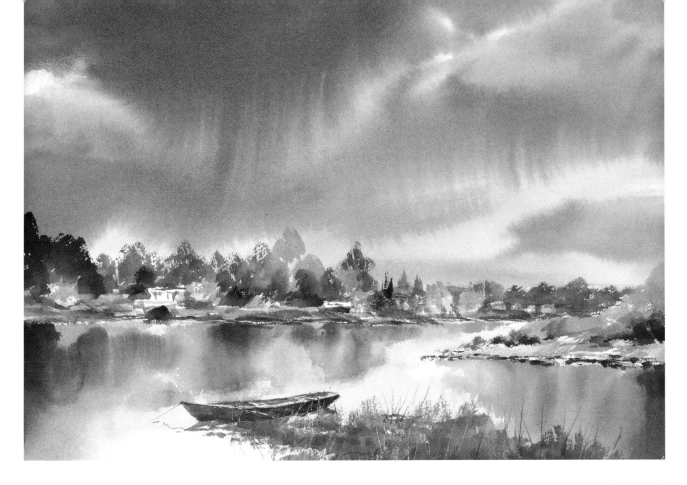

Approaching Storm over the Willamette River, Oregon, 12 x 15" (30 x 38 cm)

This painting was very exciting to tackle. While I didn't reproduce the dramatic clouds in the photograph exactly, I tried to enter into the spirit of the scene by putting in some obviously rain-bearing clouds. I kept the basic scheme of purple and orange in mind all the time and supplemented my usual palette with cadmium orange. I also used alizarin crimson and Payne's gray in the background trees to re-create the variety of lights and darks. It's probably obvious to the viewer that I reveled in creating those wet-into-wet reflections on the river.

Scottish Loch, 12 x 16" (30 x 40.5 cm)

I've dropped the horizon line in this painting, leaving more room for an interesting sky while still allowing plenty of foreground space. The soft, wet-into-wet sky creates a good foil for the more sharply defined mountains and textured rocks in the foreground. The little fishing boat has been added to give scale. Notice how the rocky peninsula points to it.

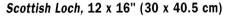

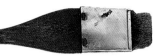

Winter Tree,
11 x 14" (28 x 35.5 cm)

In my value sketch, I removed most of the foreground shadow in the photograph on page 64, retaining some undergrowth to balance the tree. This had the effect of leading a path into the picture and through the broken wall to the trees. First I painted in a graded wash of blue sky, then the background growth, using warm and cool colors to add variation and alternation. I simplified the structure of the tree, used a hake brush to make dry brushstrokes to indicate the twigs, then painted the shadows quickly, making them less heavy than in the photograph.

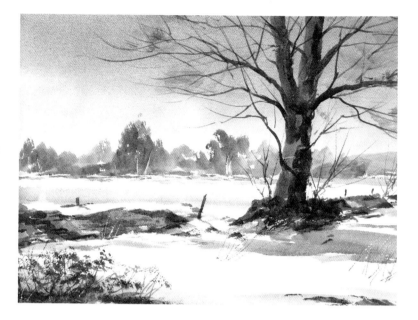

Tranquil Glade,
11 x 15"
(28 x 38 cm)

My solution to the mass of detail in the photograph was to throw the background out of focus, painting it wet-into-wet with cool colors. As I moved forward I used a richer palette. The focal point is the large tree, so I put plenty of color and texture into it. I emphasized value contrasts, putting light grasses against dark and dark against light.

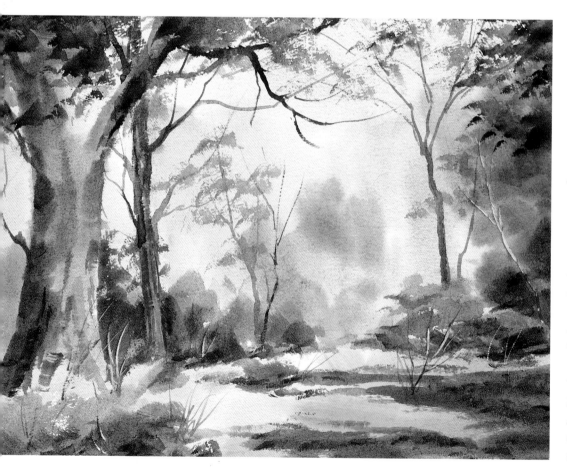

Green Symphony,
11½ x 15" (29 x 38 cm)

My first task was to paint a graded-wash sky and the background hill together, wet-into-wet. Then I mixed some rich, strong greens, made from raw sienna and ultramarine for the tree canopy in the middle distance, which I also painted before the background was dry to obtain a softened profile. On the bank below I added light red and raw sienna to warm up the area. The foreground rocks were painted with more contrast. Turning my attention to the foreground tree on the right, I painted it lightly on dry paper, but with the same mix of raw sienna and ultramarine. Notice that there is plenty of variation in the foreground at right. I scraped with the edge of a credit card to create the rocks, then, my last and most pleasurable task was to paint the river with delicate, fast brushstrokes, using lots of variation in color.

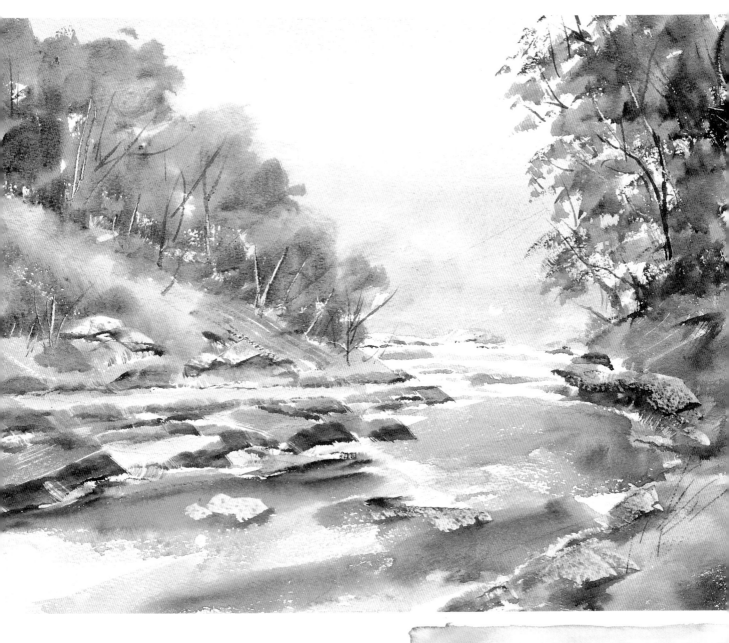

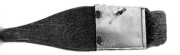

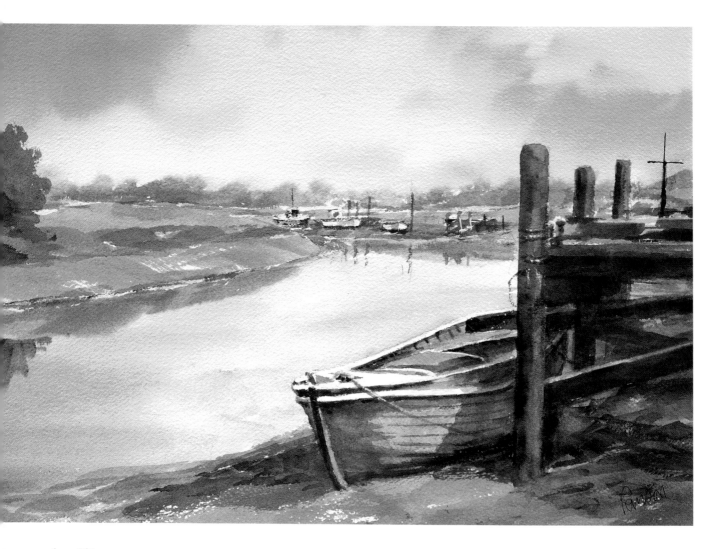

Low Tide,
11 x 14" (28 x 35.5 cm)

The four posts on the right of the page 78 photo were too distracting and took the eye away from the boat. However, because they are a good link between earth and sky, I didn't wish to remove them altogether. Instead, I shortened them, which much improved the composition but still retained their important linking function. To improve the
balance, I created a tree together with its reflection on the left side of the scene and darkened the sky above it. I painted in background trees before the sky was quite dry to establish softness as contrast with the sharp outlines of the various boats. I have restricted all detail to the foreground boat, leaving the rest of the painting loose and impressionistic—another device to direct the viewer's attention to the main object of interest.

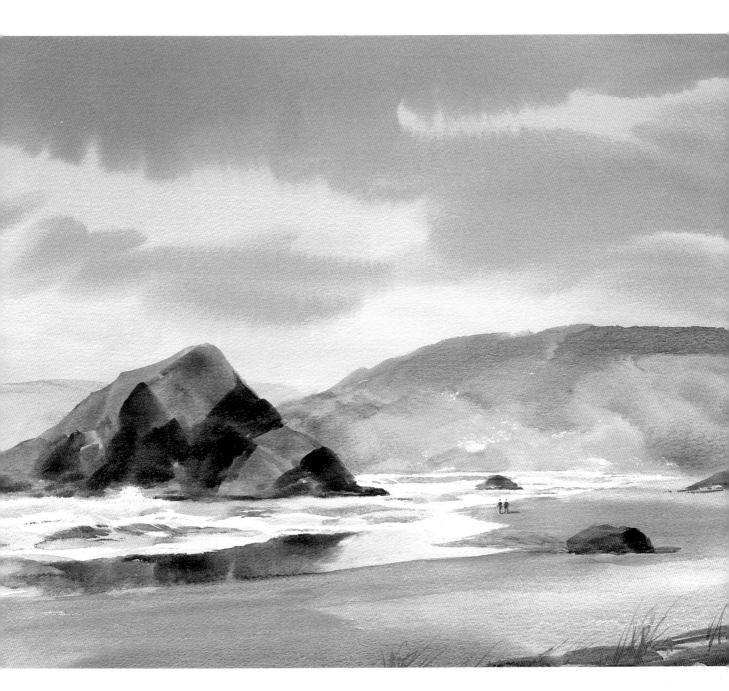

Californian Beach,
13 x 17" (33 x 43 cm)

Overlapping the rock with a distant hillside unifies this scene more satisfactorily than it was in my photo reference. I've also added a couple of figures; note that I was careful not to center them in my painting. The sky is now also more interesting than it is in the photograph, thanks to the addition of some wispy clouds and lots of Prussian blue. The background hill on the right needed color variation to make it livelier, so I added weak light red to some of the green. The large rock had to be painted quickly and freely, but I still added some purples and raw sienna for interest. Much of the ocean was left as white paper, while the stretch of foreground water mirrored the sky, but with wet-into-wet reflections. Although I did not follow all the contours when painting the sand, I did try to get in as much color variation as possible.

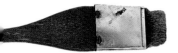

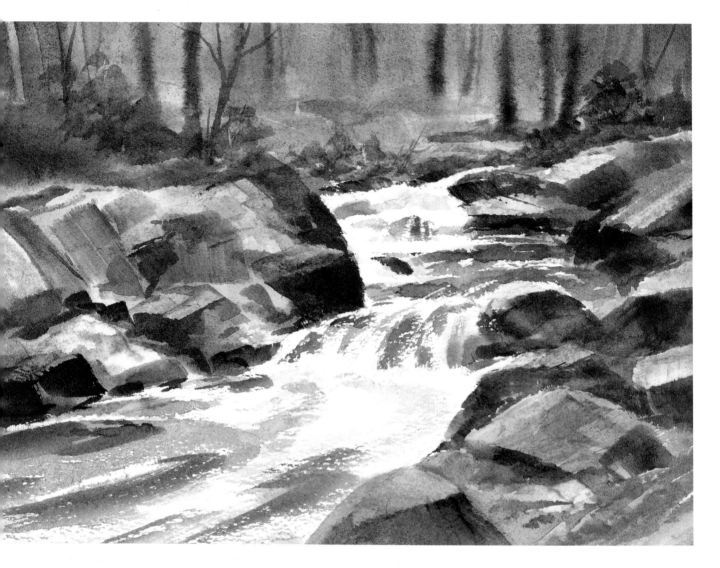

Welsh Waterfall,
9 x 13" (23 x 33 cm)

The challenge here was to portray the movement of fast-flowing water by using quick strokes of the hake and leaving plenty of white paper. I wanted to focus the viewer's attention on the water, so I subdued surrounding features. However, for added interest I put more colors into the rocks than were apparent in my reference photograph. I removed rocks that jut into the frame at the bottom of the photo, blocking an immediate view of the water. Notice how I've thrown the background woods into soft focus by using wet-into-wet technique to bring a feeling of depth to the picture and create contrast with the hard-edged foreground rocks.

**Springtime Bouquet,
10 x 9" (25.5 x 23 cm)**

I made no attempt here to paint individual flowers; the aim was to convey richness of color and strong contrast between flowers and foliage. I've varied foliage hues to avoid monotony, and added more flowers on the left. The flower colors are various combinations of lemon yellow and alizarin crimson. I've also simplified the bowl itself, using wet-into-wet application. With these flower paintings, freshness and spontaneity is all.

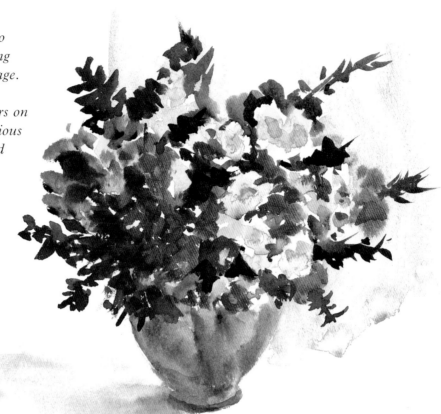

**Smoke Bush with Roses,
8 x 10" (20.5 x 25.5 cm)**

Here I put in a wet-into-wet background of pinks and orange. I also used the same colors more strongly to paint the roses, giving just a vague indication of their petals. As the paper dried I introduced much stronger greens and copper, varying the foliage palette and using hard and soft edges to show up the roses. The cut-glass container is merely hinted at. I decided before I started painting that the golden rose on the left was to be the star of the show, so I lightened it considerably and darkened leaves around it to emphasize its importance. Finally, I added a few rigger strokes to indicate stems.

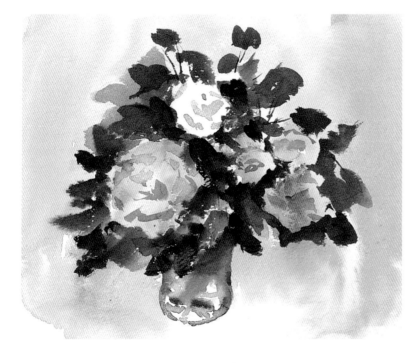

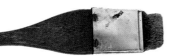

Silk Fantasy,
14 x 11" (35.5 x 28 cm)

This is really a wild-flower painting. I dampened the whole area behind the flowers, using mixes of alizarin crimson and ultramarine. The greens are mixes of lemon yellow and Payne's Gray. I repeated this medley of color as the paper dried so that the top hues are sharper while those underneath are diffused. Little attempt was made to use the reference photo, which was really only a jumping-off point. The container was painted in wet-into-wet and stems were put in with my rigger once the paper was completely dry.

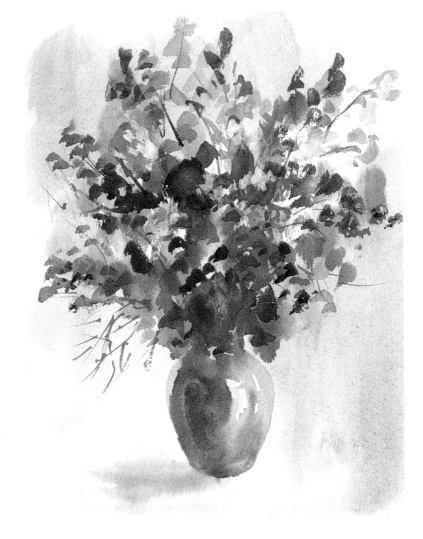

Midsummer Madness,
11½ x 15" (28.5 x 38 cm)

For this painting I arranged the figures in an arc to unify them. I placed them on one side of the picture and balanced them by putting in a dark patch of sand on the other side. I eliminated facial features completely, trying only to portray figures in action. The shadows helped greatly. Two of the figures are actually the same child; I've simply changed the clothing. I've put more variation of color into the beach than was present in the photograph.

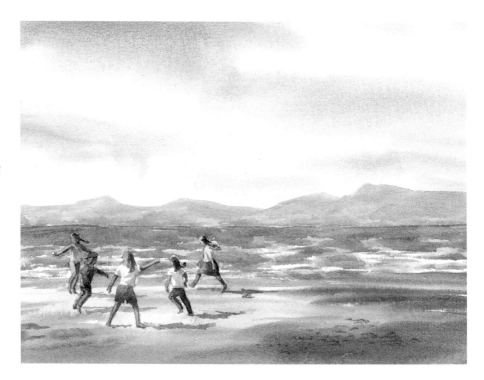

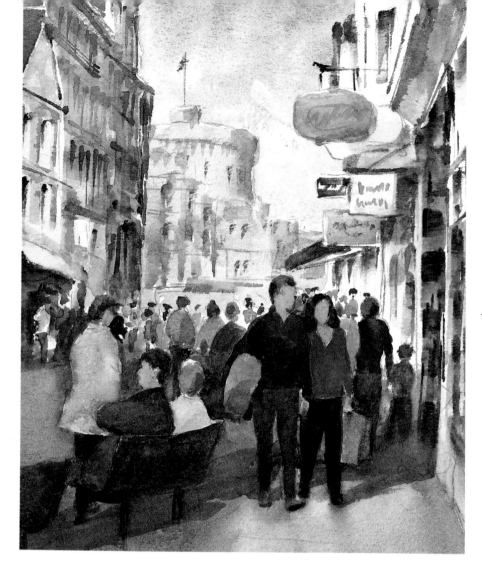

**Shopping in Windsor,
10 x 7" (25.5 x 18 cm)**

First, I painted in the sky area that defined the building profiles, then used a large, flat brush to paint all the architecture. I left white paper for the lights, but added color on some of the signs. I painted figures with a rigger, using stronger colors for those in the foreground. I chose to leave out the stroller, but added a child.

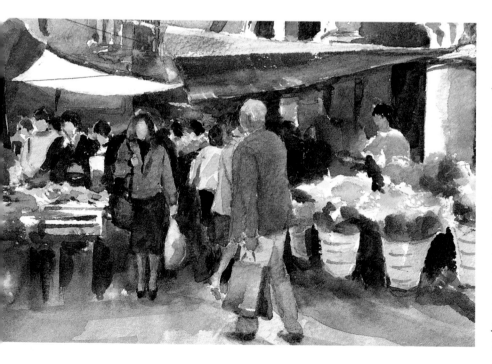

**Flower Market, Venice,
9 x 12" (23 x 30 cm)**

Again I've eliminated all facial features, and treated the produce on sale as simple patches of color. I've also reduced all architectural detail. I've made the whole scene sunnier and more sparkling than in the photograph, and brightened the paving. It's not an easy subject to paint, but simplification is a big help here. Notice how the brightened figure on the far right helps to balance the picture.

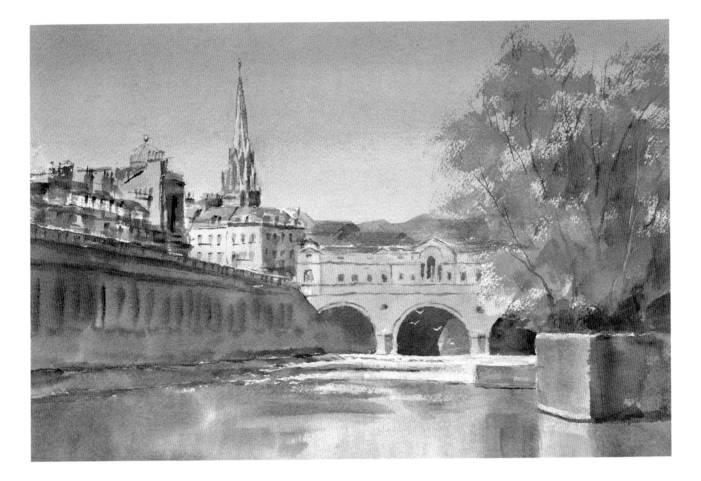

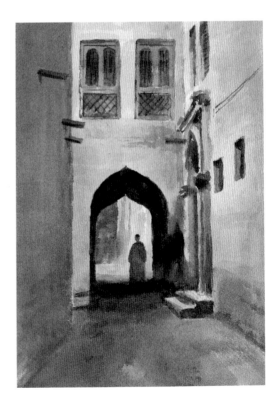

▶ *Back Street in Muscat,*
12 x 8½" (30 x 21.5 cm)

*The drama of the shadowy arch in this scene demanded a
figure, so I added one. A painting of this kind requires more
color than is evident in the photograph. For heightened
interest and variety, I strengthened both color and tonal
gradation, especially on the ground and in the left wall. I
cleared away debris at the back of the alleyway to give more
dominance to the figure, and also omitted modern, distracting
details such as electricity cables on the right wall and water
pipes on the left.*

◀ **Spring Morning in Bath,**
10 x 14" (25.5 x 35.5 cm)

As always, the sky went in first after I had masked out the profiles of buildings. To paint the columns on the left I used a dark wash and then painted areas between the columns in a darker tone still. All other detail was put in with the corner or flat edge of a 1" (25 mm) flat brush. The trees were painted in quickly, using the hake, the rigger, and a fingernail. Many of the shadows are a mixture of ultramarine and light red, and the water incorporates all surrounding colors. I used white gouache to indicate the seagulls.

▼ **Fish Market, Venice,**
9½ x 13" (24 x 33 cm)

First I darkened the sky to pick out the profiles of buildings. I painted all the buildings on the right in one wash, introducing various colors into the wet surface. I used dark, negative shapes for the fish market to show up the pillars and railings. A rich wash of light red and burnt umber was used for brickwork, then bright colors for the figures to draw attention to them. Last came the wet-into-wet reflections in the water.

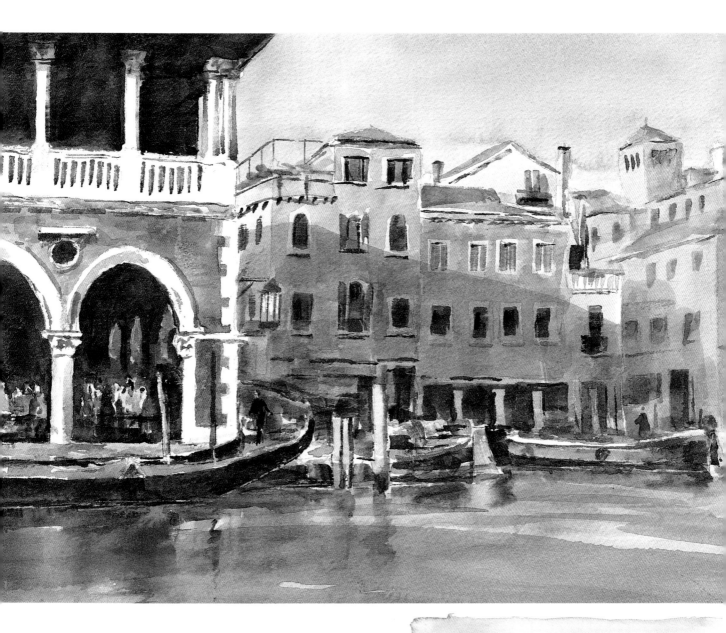

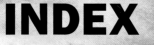

INDEX